Science That Colonizes

A Critique of Fertility Studies in Africa

In the series
Health, Society, and Policy,
edited by
Sheryl Ruzek and
Irving Kenneth Zola

Science That Colonizes

A Critique of

Fertility Studies

in Africa

Agnes Riedmann

 **Temple**
University Press
Philadelphia

Temple University Press, Philadelphia 19122
Copyright © 1993 by Temple University. All rights reserved
Published 1993

Printed in the United States of America
The paper used in this publication meets the minimum
requirements of American National Standard for Information
Sciences—Permanence of Paper for Printed Library Materials,
ANSI Z39.48-1984 ∞

The passage from Daniel Chirot and Thomas D. Hall's
"World System Theory," appearing on page 10, is reproduced,
with permission, from the Annual Review of Sociology, Vol. 8,
ed. R. Turner and J. Short, © 1982 by Annual Reviews Inc.

Library of Congress Cataloging-in-Publication Data
    Riedmann, Agnes Czerwinski.
        Science that colonizes : a critique of fertility studies
    in Africa / Agnes Riedmann.
            p.   cm.
        Includes bibliographical references and index.
        ISBN 1-56639-042-7(cl)
        1. Demographic surveys—Nigeria—
    Methodology.   2. Fertility, Human—Nigeria.
        3. Yoruba (African people)—Population.   I. Title.
    HB849.49.R54   1993
    304.6'32'072—dc20   92-26098
                                                                        CIP

To my mother
and
to my lifelong friends
from ANU

The new baby was made to taste water first.
People were curious as to its sex
They used light to check its sex,
And it was a babv-boy,
Whose profession would be game-hunting.
It is the ninth day of birth,
Let us perform birth rites so as to put the baby in peace.
Let us get ready table-salt,
Get ready red palm-oil,
Get ready honey,
The baby's alligator-pepper,
The baby's brown and light kolanuts,
A good aro fish.
To appease death and illness, water is often used.
Alcohol puts humans in good form.
Get ready soil on which I always step.
I hope all ritual materials are complete?
Thieves are characteristically quick.
Rather than hot like stirred yam flour, pounded yam is good
    if moderately hot.
Let us perform the ritual for the new baby.

Traditional testimony sung at a
Yoruba birth ceremony

The object of the feast is to introduce the baby and to name it. Like all real West Africans, the Yorubans are very fond of little children, and the ugly and, in ordinary estimation, insignificant little horror is handed round from one to another, cuddled and dandled.

From Leo Frobenius's description of a Yoruba birth ceremony, 1913

I think we should leave her as she is.
CAFN fieldworker

Do not say that what is bad is good,
Let us start climbing the tree from its trunk;
So that we may be blessed.

From an Arofo, *an ancient Yoruba poem in the oral tradition*

Contents

Maps and Tables

Acknowledgments

Sincere thanks go to the Fulbright Foundation, to John C. Caldwell and Pat Caldwell, and to the Department of Demography, Research School of Social Sciences, Australian National University, for the opportunity to spend the calendar year 1988 studying the Changing African Family–Nigeria (CAFN) data. Shortly after my arrival at ANU, Professor Caldwell suggested I "get into the Changing African Family data." With the CAFN projects, the Caldwells significantly modified demography's "normal science" research paradigm. For one thing, they developed the questionnaire in Yoruba, the respondents' language, and only later translated it to English. In addition, they incorporated a large proportion of unstructured questions and required fieldworkers to provide a vast amount of qualitative data.

Increasingly, the Caldwells have espoused a more anthropological research design in which investigators—in addition to surveying large numbers of people—live among and mingle with subjects. Furthermore, convinced that "statistics represent complex people, not simple abstractions" (see Appendix B, #47)—and that realizing those statistics is a complicated process—the Caldwells saved virtually all CAFN background documents.

Initially, I studied these documents in order to gain familiarity with the projects. Only gradually did I come to see the documents, along with the interview schedules themselves, as social products—as data for the grounded theoretical analysis on which this book is based. Although he granted me permission to use his data in this way, Professor Caldwell has asked me to point out that I developed the views presented here virtually without his knowledge and that, in fact, he had assumed that I was working on a very different topic

xiii

while I was at ANU: namely, the use of grounded theory for the study of Yoruba fertility and fertility control. Moreover, he remains unconvinced that either he or his collaborators were unwittingly the playthings of great forces of which they were largely unaware.

Thanks go to the entire staff and to all the students at ANU —especially A. Dharmalingam, Bob and Heather Hogg, Ahmet Icduygu, Roberto Rodrigues, and P. N. Sushama—who befriended and helped me.

Here in the United States, I thank Lynn K. White, Robert Benford, Suzanne Ortega, David Brinkerhoff, and Oyekan Owomoyela at the University of Nebraska; and Sheryl Ruzek, Irving Kenneth Zola, Janet Francendese, Mary Capouya, and Patricia Sterling at Temple University Press.

And special thanks to my mother, Ann Langley Czerwinski, Ph.D., Professor Emeritus, Creighton University, who supported and encouraged me in all ways, among them proofreading the manuscript.

Science That Colonizes
A Critique of
Fertility Studies
in Africa

1   Introduction
World-System
Demography
and the Yoruba

In 1985 the government of Nigeria produced a draft of that nation's first population policy statement. One of its stated objectives was "to provide to everyone the necessary information and education on the value of reasonable family size to both the individual family and the future of the nation" (Federal Republic of Nigeria, 1985: 12–13). But what *is* "reasonable" family size in Nigeria? According to the policy statement, the government's aim was to persuade as many as half of Nigeria's women, by the year 2000, to bear only four children each. Twenty years earlier, a pamphlet titled "Family Planning in Christian Marriage," published by the Christian Council of Nigeria (1965: 9, 13), had argued that "three or four" children would be reasonable.

In the early 1970s, among the majority of the Yoruba (an ethnic group constituting about 20 percent of the population of Nigeria), reasonable family size meant the greatest possible number of children a woman could bear, given that she obeyed sexual abstinence norms of some 3 years or more of postnatal abstinence and terminal abstinence beginning between the ages of 40 and 44 (Caldwell and Caldwell, 1977). In 1973 demographer John C. Caldwell settled on 5 live births as an operational definition for an "achieved small family"

1

among the Yoruba because such a small number of families had fewer than 5 children.

The social construction of reasonable family size, then—along with the necessary reconstruction of family size as an objective over which individuals appropriately take control—is in process. Moreover, First World–orchestrated fertility research undertaken in the Third World plays a part—along with Western education, media, and more direct propaganda campaigns—in that process.

Bureaucratic Surveillance

The authority of First World scientists to penetrate Third World areas for the purpose of gathering information is a carryover from the "right-to-invade" established in the fifteenth century and thereafter by musket-bearing Europeans. Modern global power, having been massively expanded by penetrating European powers during the eighteenth and nineteenth centuries (Giddens, 1987: 174–76), rests upon and employs a contemporary musket: bureaucratic administration and organization. The right-to-invade became a right to establish "bureaucratic surveillance."

Bureaucratic surveillance entails "the collection and organization of information that can be stored by agencies or collectivities and can be used to 'monitor' the activities of an administered population" (Giddens, 1987: 174). Bureaucracy "is a power instrument of the first order for one who controls the bureaucratic apparatus" (Weber, 1968; vol. 3: 987). Bureaucratic surveillance constitutes "disciplinary power" to control subordinates within the bureaucracy and others as well (Foucault, 1975).

Unlike that of preindustrial times, social control is no longer effected typically—or only—by means of physical or military violence (Foucault, 1975). Sparked by early capitalism's requirement that workers be organized and disciplined, surveillance became both bureaucratically organized and widespread (Foucault, 1975; Giddens, 1987: 176). In Max Weber's words, the eighteenth century witnessed "the advance of the rational bureaucratic structure of domination" (1968, vol. 3: 998).

Bureaucratic surveillance, still relatively weak in late-eighteenth-

and early-nineteenth-century transitional Europe (Giddens, 1987: 174), initially characterized industrialized, not traditional, societies. In the latter, social control was family or kinship centered; monitoring took the form of family (often extended-family) surveillance (Shorter, 1976; Stone, 1977). Modernization theorists typically argue that Westernization involves a shift toward individualistic values. In Third World nations the shift to individualism, understood as the potential for self-actualization, has become evident in the decline in arranged marriages and an increase in "love" matches, along with the weakening of parental control. But modernization involves a second, less apparent, and more insidious shift: an increased tolerance of bureaucratic surveillance. That the subject or unit of such surveillance is the individual masks the fact that Third World actors are not always or simply following a "wish to be free" (Shorter, 1976: 259), the motive for the move toward individualism in transitional Europe. First World–Third World encounters do not necessarily liberate the individual from family surveillance so much as move him or her from family to bureaucratic surveillance.

Compliance in bureaucratic surveillance means being willing to interact with and provide personal information to sometimes unfamiliar, nonfamily bureaucratic workers. Nigerians' compliance in bureaucratic surveillance, at least for demographic data-gathering purposes, has tended to be meager. The registration of vital statistics was initiated by the colonial government as early as 1863, yet available evidence suggests that as late as 1977, perhaps only 8 percent of births and 2 percent of deaths were registered. National legislation made registration of births and deaths compulsory in 1979, but cooperation has been minimal and enforcement less than effective, particularly in rural regions (World Fertility Survey, 1984: 5).

Demographers and government policymakers view respondents' compliance in bureaucratic surveillance as necessary to the decline of fertility in the Third World. For one thing, they tend to see such surveillance as fundamental to policy planning, since without it there are no reliable national data. Moreover, bureaucratic surveillance is integral to potential state enforcement of birth control. In its 1985 National Development Plan, the Nigerian National Planning Office "regarded the need to make a serious beginning at generating adequate and reliable population data for planning and decision-making as one of its 'over-riding objectives' " (World Fertility Survey, 1984: 5). Motivated by the absence of such data, Nigeria's federal government participated in the 1981–82 World Fertility Survey conducted by the International Statistical Institute.

Almost a decade earlier, however, in 1973, three large-scale fertility investigations were carried out among the Yoruba of western Nigeria: the Changing African Family–Nigeria (CAFN) projects. It is the background documents of these projects that this book analyzes.

The CAFN Projects

The Yoruba constitute one of three major ethnic groups in Nigeria, which is located on the Gulf of Guinea along Africa's west coast, just north of the equator; they live chiefly in the western region of the country (see Map 1). The CAFN projects were directed by Australian demographer John C. Caldwell, with Professor Francis O. Okediji of the University of Ibadan, Nigeria, serving as codirector. They were funded by a United States organization, the Population Council. The Sociology Department at the University of Ibadan was the base for the projects; assistance was provided by the Australian National University's Department of Demography. Map 2 shows the survey locations—all in the western region of Nigeria—stratified by the population size of each site. In all, 10,111 Yorubas were interviewed.

The initial purpose of the research was to investigate the preconditions of fertility decline in Africa, an aim later amended to examine conditions of stable high fertility that tend to resist the onset of fertility decline.[1] Western-educated, bilingual Yorubas were employed as middle-level staff and fieldworkers (Okediji et al., 1976: 134).

The projects were chronologically developed and designed to answer three related research questions. The first (CAFN1) was to investigate the preconditions of fertility decline in Nigeria. It was because early findings suggested that there had been virtually no onset of fertility decline that the research aim was amended in CAFN2 to examine conditions of stable high fertility that tended to resist the

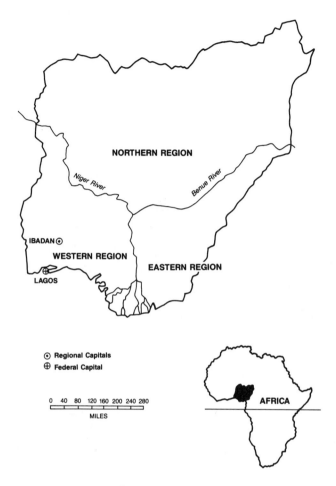

NORTHERN REGION

Niger River

Benue River

IBADAN ⊙

WESTERN REGION

EASTERN REGION

LAGOS

⊙ Regional Capitals
⊕ Federal Capital

0   40   80   120 160 200 240 280
MILES

AFRICA

Map 1. Regions of Nigeria

onset of transition. Later, using a modified research design, CAFN3 scientists reapproached their original goal, seeking to investigate any fertility decline that *had* begun in an effort to elucidate causes. Because different ethnic groups in Nigeria could be expected to place varied meanings on the interview questions, the researchers held ethnicity constant in all three projects by interviewing only Yorubas.

CAFN1, "The Beginning of Family Limitation," aimed at measuring the incidence of purposeful fertility control and the circum-

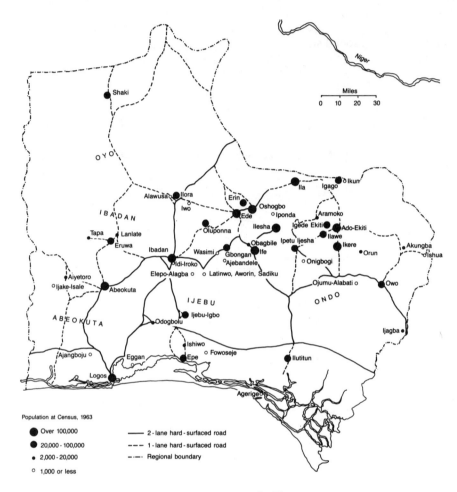

Map 2. CAFN Survey Locations Stratified by Size

stances in which it was initiated. The sampling fraction was 1 in 24 of all Yoruba females between the ages of 15 and 59 in greater Ibadan City (population, 750,000). The interview schedule consisted of two parts. Part A was administered to all subjects. Part B was administered only to those who said they had employed some method of birth control other than sexual abstinence. Part A interviews were obtained from 6,606 women. Just under one-sixth, or 1,050 women, answered Part B.

CAFN2, "The Value of Children," was designed to investigate the economic and social supports of persistent high fertility in two Nigerian states populated chiefly by Yorubas: Western State and Lagos State. Researchers hoped to secure 3,000 interviews, evenly divided by sex, among a sample of the Yoruba population over 17 years of age and residing in villages, towns, and cities throughout Lagos and other states in the western region; they did in fact obtain 1,497 interviews with males and 1,499 with females. Primarily, the investigation attempted to measure all the productive activities of children, both for immediate family benefit and for the outside market.

CAFN3, "The Achieved Small Family," set out to identify all Yoruba women over 40 years of age in greater Ibadan City who had purposefully kept family size to 5 live births or fewer by using any birth control practice, including sexual abstinence. "This meant visiting and investigating every household in the city (well over 100,000) to identify the 438 women (0.7 percent of Yoruba women over age 40 years) who stated they had deliberately achieved small families" (Okediji et al., 1976: 127). Husbands ($N = 71$) were also interviewed where these women were still in their first marriages (see Appendix B, #47).[2]

CAFN Documents as Social Products

My research treats CAFN documents—interview schedules, training manuals, supervisory memos to fieldworkers, and interviewers' written accounts of field experiences—as social products and examines the interaction between researchers and respondents as evidenced in those documents (Appendix B provides a detailed description of the data analyzed).

This approach—treating fertility research documents as social products and analyzing the researcher–respondent interaction evidenced in those documents—is similar to that of Aaron V. Cicourel's (1974) analysis of an Argentine fertility study, and many of our findings are similar. My analysis, however, differs in purpose from Cicourel's. He was primarily interested in how researcher–respondent interaction in Third World fertility research affected methodological and theoretical reliability and validity. I was interested in what the data reveal about First World–Third World social scientific interaction itself.

Three Assumptions

My analysis rests on three related assumptions. First, social science research is seldom, if ever, nonreactive in the same sense that natural science research can be; indeed, social science research is necessarily, albeit to varying degrees, interactive. Second, researcher–respondent relationships represent the sociocultural milieu in which they are found. Both sides in such relationships "approach their life worlds from the standpoint of typified stocks of knowledge that reflect their embodied locations in preexisting and emergent political, economic, ritual, and moral structures of crystallized social experience" (Denzin, 1983: 139). Finally, with regard to research undertaken in the Third World, those "embodied locations" have differential power within a stratified world system. While this last assumption is in some degree true for all researcher–respondent relationships, it is especially apparent in First World–Third World research.

From World-System Theory to World-System Demography

At least since the discovery of the Hawthorne effect (improved performance resulting from the awareness of being under concerned observation), social scientists have known that "observation can cause disturbance in the facts observed" (Bourgeois-Pichat, 1973: 9). Cicourel states the case strongly: "Researchers in the social sciences are faced with a unique methodological problem; the very conditions of their research constitute an important complex variable for what passes as findings of their investigations" (1974: 39). According to Anthony Giddens:

> The social sciences operate within a double hermeneutic, involving two-way ties with the actions and institutions of those they study. Sociological observers depend upon lay concepts to generate accurate descriptions of social processes; and agents regularly appropriate theories and concepts of social science within their behaviour, thus potentially changing its character. (1987: 31)

In other words, "there is constant 'slippage'" between social scientific and lay worlds of meaning (Giddens, 1984: 374). Lay actors pick up social scientific definitions of situations as these slip from the world of social science into that of everyday life. Researchers gain information from respondents—and vice versa.

Moreover, "as a form of interaction, social science clearly reflects and reproduces the wider social structure in which it is set" (Wilson, 1983: 250). Cicourel's purpose is to call into question concepts of validity and reliability in social scientific research, a goal set apart from my own. Nevertheless, his argument is important here. The methodological literature on the process and issues of interviewing, Cicourel concluded, implies that

> both interviewer and respondents can be viewed as social types and that they treat each other as such. Thus, though certain subjects and some observers can control the imputations attached to others, they cannot always control their actions or suspend the relevance of the imputations for the purpose of the brief encounter. We find that continuous situational imputations, strategies, and the like occur which influence how actors treat each other and manage their presence before each other. *Now, these are precisely the conditions found in everyday life.* (1974: 87; emphasis added)

In a critical essay on methodology, H. T. Wilson turns Cicourel's argument around and proposes an alternative way of looking at social science research practices:

> Instead of viewing these efforts exclusively or mainly as a *means* of acquiring knowledge about social structure and social interaction, I treat these activities and protocols as a *form* of social interaction expressive of certain structural and normative properties endemic to advanced industrial societies. (1983: 247; original emphasis)

Because global structural and cultural stratification is integral to research in the Third World, my analysis treats data from researchers and respondents as representative respectively of First World, or "core," and Third World, or "peripheral," categories of actors. Most readers will recognize the concepts *core* and *peripheral* as integral to "world-system theory."

In the United States, sociologist Immanuel Wallerstein (1974, 1979, 1980) named world-system theory and brought it to the fore in the 1970s. Daniel Chirot and Thomas D. Hall (1982: 89) point out the "curious and today little known fact," that world-system theory began in Latin America with what has become known as "dependency theory." Dependency theory emerged in publications from the United Nations Economic Commission for Latin America (ECLA) during the late 1940s and early 1950s. In fact, Wallerstein ascribes the terminology of "core" and "periphery" to ECLA, according to Chirot and Hall (1982: 90), who add:

> Of course, cultural imperialism being what it is, the world-system theorists from the North are now being used by Southern dependency theorists to legitimize their ideas. No more ironic illustration could exist of core domination and use of peripheral resources. The periphery can now reimport the product it originally exported, and leave behind a surplus of cultural prestige and strength in the core.

Generally, the world-system perspective holds that what is today called the Third World reached its present state by being systematically underdeveloped by First World powers (Amin, 1976; Frank, 1969, 1979; Wallerstein, 1974, 1979, 1980). Using their greater military, political, and economic power, core nations of northwestern Europe and, later, the United States orchestrated Third World changes beneficial to themselves. The result has been a "developmentally distorted periphery" (Amin, 1976: 201; Wallerstein, 1974, 1979, 1980).

A major assumption behind my research is that global stratification is not only economic but also ideational, or cultural, and that global exploitation goes beyond the obviously economic to include worldwide scientific research. To put it more specifically, fertility research in the Third World is indicative of "world-system demography."

Using data from the fertility surveys conducted in Nigeria, this study examines *world-system demography* as an agent of cultural imperialism, or First World–directed cultural imposition. World-system demography is my own concept. The term denotes current demographic practice, which (like other sciences in varying degrees) is global, bureaucratically administered, and controlled by elites within core nations. Chapter 7 examines the concept and its application more intensively.

Nigerian Demographic Data

Table 1.1 gives demographic data for Nigeria in 1976 (approximately the time of the CAFN research) and in 1991.[3] For the sake of comparison, data are presented for the United States and the world as well. With 122.5 million people in 1991, Nigeria is Africa's most populous country and the eighth largest in population in the world. According to Population Reference Bureau estimates, the total fertility rate and the crude birth rate declined in Nigeria between 1976 and 1991—from 6.9 to 6.2 and from 49 to 44 per thousand, respectively. Still, those rates remain significantly higher than the 1991 world averages of 3.4 and 27, respectively. In 1991 Nigeria's crude birth rate was almost three times that of the United States. Nigeria's annual population increase was 2.7 percent, more than three times that of the United States and significantly higher than the world's average of 1.7. In 1991, population-doubling time stood at 25 years in Nigeria, compared with 88 years in the United States and 40 years worldwide.

Moreover, Nigeria's crude death rate of 17, though having declined from 23 since 1976, was nearly twice that of the United States and the world. More dramatic, Nigeria's 1991 infant mortality rate of 119 (also having declined significantly since 1976) was thirteen times that of the United States and 175 percent of that for the world. In 1991, life expectancy at birth in Nigeria was 48 years, compared with 75 years in the United States and 65 years worldwide.

The table also gives comparative data on per capita gross national product in United States dollars for 1976 and 1991. Per capita share of the gross national product (GNP) is one indicator of national wealth as measured within a global money economy. In 1976, when its oil exports were bringing high returns, Nigeria's per capita GNP was $240, or 3.6 percent that of the United States and 17.6 percent of the world average. Between 1980 and 1987, however, Nigeria's per capita GNP

Table 1.1. Demographic Data for Nigeria, the United States, and the World, 1976 and 1991

	1976	1991
Total population (millions)		
Nigeria	64.7	122.5
United States	215.3	252.8
World	4,019.0	5,384.0
Total fertility rate (average total children per woman at current childbearing rates)		
Nigeria	6.9	6.2
United States	1.8	2.1
World	3.7	3.4
Crude birth rate (annual births per 1,000 population)		
Nigeria	49	44
United States	15	17
World	30	27
Annual population increase (percent)		
Nigeria	2.7	2.8
United States	0.8	0.8
World	1.8	1.7
Years to double population		
Nigeria	26	25
United States	87	88
World	38	40
Crude death rate (annual deaths per 1,000 population)		
Nigeria	23	17
United States	9	9
World	12	9
Infant mortality rate (annual deaths of infants under 1 year per 1,000 live births)		
Nigeria	180	119
United States	17	9.1
World	105	68

Table 1.1. (*continued*)

	1976	1991
Life expectancy at birth (years)		
Nigeria	41	48
United States	71	75
World	59	65
Per capita gross national product (1989 US$)		
Nigeria	$240	$250
United States	6,640	21,000
World	1,360	3,760

Sources: "1976 World Population Data Sheet"; "Family Planning and Marriage 1970–1980"; "1991 World Population Data Sheet," all from the Population Reference Bureau, Washington, D.C.

The Population Reference Bureau compiles rates and figures from the following sources: United Nations, *Demographic Yearbook*; UN Statistical Office, *Population and Vital Statistics Report*; UN Population Division, *World Population Prospects as Assessed in 1990*; files of the Center for International Research, U.S. Bureau of the Census; publications of the Council of Europe and the European Communities; long-term population projections of the World Bank; recent demographic surveys, special studies, and direct communication with demographers and statistical bureaus in the United States and abroad.

declined in real terms at an estimated average of 5 percent annually ("Nigeria," 1991: 1945). In 1991 Nigeria's per capita GNP was $250, just 1.19 percent of the United States figure and 6.65 percent of the world average.

In general, Yoruba demographic data are subsumed within and approximate those for Nigeria. Nigeria's high population growth, birth, death, and infant mortality rates, together with low life expectancy and per capita GNP, typify what have come to be known as "Third World," underdeveloped, or peripheral nations within a world system.

The Yoruba

In the fifteenth and sixteenth centuries respectively, the Portuguese and the British made contact with Yoruba territories. By the sixteenth century the British had taken slaves, ivory, and pepper from

Yorubaland (originally a kingdom); later they would extract palm oil for use in soap and as a machine lubricant (Aripko, 1967; Burns, 1948; Frobenius, 1913; Isichei, 1983). Lagos, a major Yoruba coastal city (and now Nigeria's federal capital) became a slave-trading center. By the mid-nineteenth century, Christian missionaries had entered Yorubaland and established schools. After 300 years of de facto colonialization, the British officially established the Colony of Lagos in 1861. In 1914 the Crown created Nigeria by merging the Colony of Lagos with adjoining protectorates. Incidents associated with World War II catalyzed a nascent nationalism (Arikpo, 1967; Eades, 1980; Isichei, 1983), and in 1960 Nigeria became politically independent in a bloodless revolution.

Britain brought Yorubaland into a peripheralized position within the world economy, and that position persists. Like most Third World societies, the Yoruba in the 1970s—when the CAFN research was done—exhibited the juxtaposition of traditional and industrialized social structure and culture. For instance, wage labor existed alongside the subsistence occupations of farming and petty trading. Asked what kind of job they did most of the time, 35 percent of the men interviewed in CAFN2 said farming or fishing;[4] another 24 percent said they were professionals, managers, or white-collar employees,[5] and 22 percent were primarily skilled laborers. Of the women, 47 percent were petty traders[6] (indeed, market trading has long been a traditional major enterprise, particularly for Yoruba women);[7] 12 percent were professionals or white-collar workers; another 12 percent worked as skilled laborers.

Education levels, like occupations, evidenced the heterogeneity of a partly deconstructed and subsequently reconstructed society. In the early 1970s, half of the Yoruba had had no Western education. Of the remainder, about 20 percent had attended primary school for one to six years; about 10 percent had received some secondary schooling; another 7 percent (5.7 and 8.6 of women and men, respectively) had attained secondary school certificates. Nearly 5 percent (3.8 of women and 5.7 of men) had undergone teacher training; 3.3 percent (2.5 for women and 4.2 for men) had received non-university tertiary training; and 3 percent of CAFN2 respondents had attended the university: 19 women and 71 men.[8]

Like occupations and education levels, religion evidenced the juxtaposition of the imposed with the indigenous. Three-fifths of CAFN2 respondents were members of Christian denominations developed in Europe. Another one-third were Moslems. The remainder belonged to Christian churches developed in Africa during the late nineteenth century or to indigenous African religions, the latter characterized by divination, belief in reincarnation, and worship of ancestors, spirits, and various gods. Syncretism of indigenous African with Christian or Moslem religions was apparent; particularly in rural areas, indigenous beliefs and practices defined the culture (Caldwell and Caldwell 1985).

Christianity and formal schooling remained correlated among CAFN2 respondents. In 1973 nearly two-thirds of the Moslems had received no Western education; among European Protestants, however, that figure was less than one-third. Furthermore, about 80 percent of those with university or other tertiary education were Christian.

As one might expect, Western education correlated also with occupation and income. Of respondents who mostly farmed or fished, 83 percent had no formal education, and the majority reported earning little or no money. Seventy percent of petty traders and 40 percent of laborers (who typically occupy the middle incomes) had no Western schooling. Three-quarters of professional and other white-collar workers, however, had received at least a secondary school certificate. Professionals enjoyed the highest income.

Yoruba cities and towns too evidenced the juxtaposition of modernity and tradition. In 1973 Abeokuta, a city of more than 100,000 inhabitants, had a fire department, six post offices, five banks, seven hospitals, and twenty-two doctors trained in Western medicine, as well as a family planning clinic.[9] There were more than a hundred primary schools, twenty-two secondary schools, and three factories.[10] At the same time, the city had three daily markets and nearly 600 herbalists or traditional doctors. Abeokuta had a twenty-four-hour electricity supply and both in-house piped water and public taps; radios were "common in almost every house of an average person," and there was television with "good reception" but only "in the houses of the well-to-do." The city had both motor-driven sewage facilities and "channels . . . for the removal of foul liquid materials or waste organic matters." Trucks transported garbage and other refuse to specific "spots," but some was also "thrown to any nearby bush or to a public dunghill" (see Appendix B, #27).

Aiyetoro, a smaller town of fewer than 20,000 people, lies about twenty miles west of Abeokuta by a one-lane road. In 1973 Aiyetoro had both a daily market and a post office. The town also had a health center; there were "few" Western-trained doctors or other health workers but "many" midwives, herbalists, and traditional doctors. There was no electricity except in the secondary school, which maintained its own generator. Water was available only from public taps and untreated wells. There were no sewage facilities, and garbage disposal was "in the bushes." Aiyetoro had access to radio but not television broadcasts.

By the early 1970s perhaps one-half of all Yorubas lived in urban areas, with over one-fifth in Lagos and Ibadan (Caldwell, 1976a: 197–98; 1977a: 13).[11] Not surprisingly, rural areas had remained more traditional than urban centers. Villages and towns comprised largely residential, multifamily compounds: adjoining rooms surrounding an open quadrangle.[12] Compounds also existed in the older sections of Ibadan, juxtaposed with living quarters that more nearly resembled European residences (Caldwell and Caldwell, 1987: 419). Structurally and culturally, Yorubaland evidenced the heterogeneity of two worlds: "the traditional one and the modern one installed by colonization" (Amin, 1976: 220).

As is characteristic of peripheral nations, a significant proportion of Yorubas today still embody a "pseudo-traditional society integrated into the world system" (Amin, 1976: 328–29). In Yorubaland, family size values are "large family" values, and the persistence of subsistence farming (see "Nigeria," 1991: 2007) provides some economic infrastructure upon which to support large families.

Children are instrumentally valued in nonindustrialized economies because child-rearing costs are outweighed by children's productivity and the potential future security they offer as parents age (Cain, 1983; Caldwell, 1976a, 1982a, 1982b). For instance, Yoruba children run messages, carry fuel and food and water, look after younger siblings, work fields, and help with marketing and food preparation and cleaning (Caldwell, 1976a: 216–17). In Caldwell's (1982b) now classic theoretical contribution and phraseology, intergenerational wealth flow throughout the Third World is typically upward.

Yoruba culture has traditionally been—and to a significant extent remains—polygynous (Bascom, 1969; Fadipe, 1970).[13] It is a culture and society "molded by stress on ancestry and descent" (Caldwell and Caldwell, 1987: 410), with fertility matters often consciously and purposefully left "up to God." Postpartum female sexual abstinence for up to three years and permanent abstinence among grandmothers are commonly practiced not to limit reproduction but to maximize children's survival chances. The purpose of a mother's postnatal abstinence is to promote the nursing infant's health. The purpose of a grandmother's abstinence is to avoid potential conflict between grandmother and mother roles, since a woman's mother assists her at birth and aids in child care thereafter (Caldwell, 1976a; Caldwell and Caldwell, 1977 and 1987; Okediji et al., 1976). In short, "there has been no traditional fertility control in the sense of attempts to . . . call a halt to family building beyond an acceptable size" (Caldwell and Caldwell, 1987: 411). As a result, the current total fertility rate of 6.5 is among the world's highest.

What Follows

Although it proceeds from the assumptions of world-system theory, my project here is primarily one of generating grounded theory: that is, developing theory from raw data by processes of induction, deduction, verification, and integration (see Glaser and Strauss, 1967; Strauss, 1987). My study design is described in Appendix A, and the data I have analyzed—background documents from the CAFN projects—are detailed in Appendix B.

Building on the foregoing sketch of Yoruba society, the next two chapters examine the historical and structural context for bureaucratic surveillance as evidenced by the Changing African Family–Nigeria projects. Chapter 2 presents a historical overview of advancing bureaucratic surveillance from colonialization onward; Chapter 3 describes the training and motivation of Yoruba field-workers to become members of a contemporary surveillance organization, the CAFN bureaucracy. Chapters 4 through 6 present data pertaining directly to the Yoruba interviews. Chapter 4 describes the process of gaining entrance into the lives of respondents; Chapter 5 explicates the underlying messages or "lessons" inherent in CAFN; Chapter 6 illustrates ways in which some subjects resisted those lessons. Finally, Chapter 7 offers a summary discussion of CAFN and world-system demography and suggests policy issues raised by this research.

2　　Historical Prelude
Bringing Yorubaland
into the World
System

By the mid-fifteenth century, seafaring Portuguese were exploring the West African coast and had taken slaves, ivory, and pepper. British ships first reached what is now Nigeria in 1553 and within thirty days had collected eighty tons of pepper. Over the following four centuries the British colonial government removed cargoes not only of pepper but also of slaves ("shipped by the grace of God," it was said), ivory, palm oil, textiles, priceless art, and artifacts (Burns, 1948: 63–66; see also Waddell, 1960; Wallerstein, 1980: 270–71). Initially, Nigerians compared the British to locusts: they were devastating, but they would go away (Temple, 1918). When they did not, resistance emerged.

Historical events in Yorubaland both foreshadowed and helped create the environment in which the Changing African Family–Nigeria research took place. This chapter explores four continuing themes evidenced in that history and relates them to the CAFN projects: (1) Eurocentric devaluation of the Yoruba, (2) destruction of the indigenous social structure and culture by deconstructing the economy; (3) orchestration of change from without via advancing bureaucratic surveillance; and (4) indigenous resistance to foreign penetration.

Eurocentric Devaluation of the Yoruba

European explorers typically saw Africans as less civilized than they. "If a torrid climate engendered torrid emotions, as was conventionally assumed, the African might be expected to have the fieriest temperament of all" (Kiernan, 1969: 196). Britain's Sir Alan Burns, writing his *History of Nigeria* in 1929, praised the "brave" British, who "had to undergo dangers from a hostile and fanatical population" (1948: 96). In a later work, *In Defence of Colonies* (1957: 42), Burns argued that "at its lowest assessment British rule was the lesser of two evils." Typically, the European invader was quick to define culture traits such as polygyny, facial scarring, divination, and human sacrifice as savage or subhuman. In the words of one village elder, however, "no human being could be so wicked" as the "white things" who, for example, set villages on fire at will (quoted in Isichei, 1983: 376).

Devaluation involved a failure to impute equal intelligence or talent to Yorubas and Europeans. For example, in 1910 the German anthropologist Leo Frobenius discovered the now world-famous terra-cotta, bronze, and brass sculptures of Ife, Yorubaland, dated about 800 to 1000 A.D. The quality of the Ife art was so high, it was felt (in a theory no longer tenable), that it could not possibly have been created by ancestors of the twentieth-century inhabitants (Smith, 1969: 13). Frobenius (1913) suggested that the sculptures must have been the work of an immigrant Greek colony (see also Isichei, 1983: 345). Burns later argued that the Portuguese must have taught the Yoruba (1948: 64).

Devaluation was further evident in colonialists' overall lack of respect for Yorubas and Yoruba property. The men of Britain's late-nineteenth-century Royal Niger Company, for example, soon acquired a local reputation for disorder, dishonesty, cruelty, and general bad manners. For one thing, they felt free to pillage local villages, "catching goats, fowls and cows at will for their food and pleasure" (Isichei, 1983: 364). A missionary recorded the response of the indigenes to the Niger Company: "How fully they believe that the White Traders are untrustworthy and that their country would be richer if all the white men were banished" (quoted in Isichei, 1983: 365).

As time passed and some Yorubas became formally educated and otherwise Westernized, colonialists saw them mainly as "comic" or "infernally bumptious" (in Isichei, 1983: 391) or as "character-less mulattoes" (in McIntyre, 1967: 114). Frobenius sniggered at the "trousered black gentry" with their "ridiculous affectations" (1913: 41, 270). Moreover, devaluation meant blanket disregard for indigenous culture, so that major institutions were changed—whether willfully or by chance—without qualm.

Deconstruction of the Indigenous Economy

Europeans' need for raw materials and export markets had "stimulated the taste for adventure" (Maunier, 1949: 12). Worldwide, colonialization was characterized by the wholesale extraction of indigenous resources; Yorubaland was no exception. Frobenius boasted about the wealth that found its way to European harbors in exchange "for a mere song": that is, "empty bottles, trouser buttons, or frayed epaulettes" (1913: 50–55). Throughout the colonial period, palm oil was increasingly in European demand as a fuel, a soap ingredient, and, later, a motor lubricant (Isichei, 1983: 98). As a result, British merchants—or "palm oil ruffians," as they were known among the indigenes (Arikpo, 1967: 30; Isichei, 1983: 327)—cheaply extracted palm oil from groves along the mouths of the "oil rivers." By the 1860s the value of palm oil imported by Great Britain was estimated at over a million pounds annually (McIntyre, 1967: 82).

Besides the extraction of raw materials, the indigenous economy was damaged by imports. Precolonial blacksmiths had fashioned hoes, bolts, bells, and body jewelry (Fadipe, 1970: 153) and, later, modeled flintlock guns after European firearms. But by the 1950s, indigenous iron smelting and working had disappeared, primarily as a result of imported metal products (Biobaku, 1973: 144–46; Isichei, 1983; Johnson, 1966: 119ff). Isichei sees this as "one of the classic examples in world history of de-industrialization caused by colonialism" (1983: 50; see also Biabaku, 1973: 144–49). Deindustrialization characterized salt and cloth production as well.

"But there was a more fundamental inequality in the exchange," Elizabeth Isichei points out. African labor created wealth in Europe and the New World. In return, African communities received products such as brandy, gin, and guns, which were not only potentially destructive but were soon consumed or worn out and offered no stimulus for production or technological advance. Most imports were luxury items "marginal to the economy of the societies which paid such a heavy price for them. . . . Sometimes it seemed as if generations of Atlantic trade had left southern Nigeria little better than an expensive junk heap" (1983: 103).

Not only industry but crafts suffered under colonialism.[1] For example, the production of elaborately decorated calabashes and pottery water coolers dwindled with the advent of piped water, imported metal or plastic containers, and refrigeration (O'Hear, 1986). Intricate wood carving declined along with the traditional religion for which most carvings were made (Eades, 1980: 85).[2]

Furthermore, by the early twentieth century the Crown was encouraging colonial cash crop production for European markets. Cocoa, introduced as an export crop in Yorubaland in about 1900 (Eades, 1980: 65–66), remains a principal Nigerian export. Previously, probably 60 percent of men were hunters, simultaneously engaging in subsidiary farming (Ojo, 1966).[3] But as rain forests, habitat for game, were cleared—not only to make way for the new crop but also to supply an export timber industry—diminished hunting areas meant the demise of that principal occupation (Ojo, 1966: 42–43).

Cocoa changed not only hunting but also farming, albeit not so completely. Land, traditionally held in common, was never alienated de jure in Yorubaland but often became alienated de facto, because a cocoa enterpreneur could own the trees if not the ground itself (Bascom, 1969: 18; Eades, 1980: 66–67; Fadipe, 1970: 175). As a result, at least from about 1950, land available for subsistence farming decreased significantly. Cacao trees now cover so much land that some rural areas must import yams and other food previously grown locally (Caldwell, 1976a: 197–98; 1977a: 12–13). As game habitat and farmland dwindled, colonialists introduced wage occupations, further undermining both farming and the traditional craft apprentice system (Fadipe, 1970: 92).

In the early twentieth century much of this wage labor was compulsory. Under the 1923 Roads and Rivers Ordinance, for example, the colonial governor could direct that any road or river be kept clean by indigenous laborers. By 1927 that ordinance had been repealed, yet compulsory labor was still exacted in connection with public works such as railway and road construction (Buell, 1928: 657–59). Britain further "stimulated" the development of a cash economy by taxing Yorubas in money. Initiated in 1918, taxation in money virtually necessitated wage labor (Buell, 1928: 657–59, 709; Fadipe, 1970: 215; Trenchard, 1987: 156).[4]

Once Nigeria had been brought into a world economy, economic indicators rose and fell according to conditions beyond indigenous control. In 1934, for example, the price paid for palm oil fell to only one-third of what it had been a decade before. Depression and wide unemployment followed (Fadipe, 1970: 93). Forty years later, burgeoning petroleum sales created an economic boom; then in 1982 the global oil glut pulled Nigeria into an unprecedented recession from which the country has not yet recovered (Goliber, 1989: 33; "Nigeria," 1991: 1946).[5]

Colonialization, legitimized by Eurocentric devaluation of the Yoruba, deconstructed the indigenous economy and reconstructed Nigeria as peripheral in a centralized world system.

> Traditional society was distorted to the point of being unrecognizable; it lost its independence, and its main function was now to produce for the world market under conditions which, because they impoverished it, deprived this society of any prospect of radical modernization. This traditional society was not, therefore, in transition to modernity; as a dependent, peripheral society it was complete, and hence a dead end; its progress blocked. (Amin, 1976: 328)

Advancing Bureaucratic Surveillance

Only about 27,000 non-Africans live in Nigeria today among a population of more than 122 million. The hot, humid climate coupled with deadly tropical diseases (sleeping sickness, dysentery, fevers, malaria) deterred early white settlement and led colonialists to dub the Guinea Coast "White Man's Grave" (Bascom, 1969: 4–5). C. L.

Temple, a British official in Nigeria in 1918, found the region so un-healthy for Europeans that "no part of it can ever become a 'white man's' country" (1918: 11). He recommended eighteen months as a maximum stay. One result was that Britain administered Yorubaland from without by training indigenes as bureaucratic subordinates.

Official English political penetration of Yorubaland began in 1849 with the appointment of Crown consuls in the region. This action was taken in response to the repeated requests of British merchants for Crown protection from indigenous acts of rebellion (Arikpo, 1967: 30). The first Crown consul was John Beecroft, who proved "a masterly exponent of 'informal empire'" (McIntyre, 1967: 89).[6]

Over the next several years the strategic value of Lagos as a com-mercial center and gateway to the interior gradually became clear. Hence, in 1853 marines attacked and, after four days of fighting, cap-tured Lagos (Arikpo, 1967: 32; Burns, 1948: 120). But in the absence of large numbers of colonial inhabitants, occupation was tenuous, and struggle for the control of Lagos continued.

Then in 1861 England's secretary of foreign affairs instructed the Crown consul to arrange for the occupation of Lagos. Armed marines accompanied British officials to a conference with the indigenous King Dosumu, who ultimately signed what became known as the Treaty of Cession. Under the treaty, Dosumu transferred the port and island of Lagos, "together with rights, profits, territories and appur-tenances thereunto attached," to the British Crown in return for an annual pension and the rights to continue the use of his title and to decide (subject to appeal to British laws) disputes among Lagos indigenes (Arikpo, 1967: 31–32). Dosumu had signed away his tradi-tional authority to become a subordinate in the advancing colonial bureaucracy.

The Subordination of Local Leaders

By the 1880s, France and Germany had gained footholds in western Africa. The British feared that foreign colonialization might mean the eventual expulsion of Crown merchants. To avoid this, they under-took a series of "treaties of peace, friendship, and commerce" with local chiefs (Isichei, 1983: 363). In 1886 the governor of the Colony of Lagos persuaded the rulers of Oyo and Ife, along with several lesser Yoruba chiefs, to sign the first of many such treaties (Arikpo, 1967: 33). The Yoruba leaders agreed to submit to any "necessary or expedient" directives from the Lagos colonial government and to refer disputes to arbitration by the governor of Lagos.

Reducing indigenous leaders to bureaucratic subordinates proved effective. The colony gradually enlarged so that by 1893 it included the whole of the territory between Lagos and the Cameroons border to the south and extended northward along the Niger; it became known as the Niger Coast Protectorate (Arikpo, 1967). The last fifteen years of the nineteenth century marked Nigeria's "final loss of sovereignty" (Ifemisia, 1978). With the continued use of similar treaties, virtually the whole region came under what Burns (1948: 132) saw as the beginnings of an "ordered administration."

On January 1, 1900, Britain merged the Niger Coast Protectorate with the Royal Niger Company's jurisdiction to form the Protectorate of Southern Nigeria. In November 1913 Britain brought under one general government the Protectorate of Southern Nigeria and the previously established Protectorate of Northern Nigeria. Finally, on New Year's Day, 1914, a new political entity known as the Colony and Protectorate of Nigeria—or Nigeria for short—appeared on the world map "in the red shading of the British Empire" (Arikpo, 1967: 37).[7] Advancing and increasingly centralized bureaucracy had won the territory for England.

As time went on, British bureaucratic control rendered the indigenous political system virtually impotent. According to legend, precolonial Yorubaland had been divided into fourteen kingdoms, each ruled by an *oba*, or king. Many of these kingdoms had had sophisticated systems of government that included palace police; subsidiary *bales*, or chiefs; a judiciary; and various politico-religious, occupational, and mutual help associations (Bascom, 1969: 36–37; Fadipe, 1970: 198–210, 243–60; Frobenius, 1913: 56–57). Sources of government revenue included tolls collected at town gates, court fees, fines, patronage and other taxes (Fadipe, 1970: 219–22). These were paid in kind; for example, successful hunters might present to their local oba the skin of the leopard, the tail and ivory of the elephant, or the tail feather of the egret (Ojo, 1966: 38).

Throughout the first half of the twentieth century, British-controlled bureaucratic surveillance deconstructed these systems. The 1923 Native Authority Ordinance initiated a network of indigenous law enforcement authorities whose mission it was to "maintain order and good government." By 1945 several hundred such authorities had been established (Arikpo, 1967: 45). In addition, a Native Courts Ordinance called for a network of indigenous courts to administer "native law and custom . . . to the extent that it was not regarded as being repugnant to natural justice and morality" (quoted in Arikpo, 1967: 45). This meant that decisions could be reviewed by or appealed to British colonial officers (Buell, 1928: 649–52).

Many appointed native authorities and court personnel were chiefs or obas who had been bankrupted by the changing economy (Fadipe, 1970: 215). They were paid from centrally administered tax revenues. Beside mitigating their power, paying chiefs and obas from tax revenues tended to divorce their allegiance from the Yoruba people (Fadipe, 1970: 216). Moreover, the fact that records were kept in English demanded the employment of British-educated Yoruba clerks, who "in many cases usurped the authority of the real chiefs" (Buell, 1928: 691–92).

The Education of Indigenes

Before the British outlawed slavery, European dealers were known sometimes to arrange for coastal chiefs' sons to go to school in England (Kiernan, 1969: 202). But the main impetus for the emergence of a bilingual educated class had to do with Britain's efforts to abolish slave carrying. In 1807 the British Parliament passed an act prohibiting the transport of slaves in British ships (Burns, 1948: 73; Webster, 1964). A year later, England placed a naval squadron in the Guinea Gulf to interfere with the continuing Spanish and Portuguese slave trade. The British intercepted slave ships, forcing them ashore. There, in Church Missionary Society (CMS) schools, the freed slaves received industrial training along with education in English so that they could read the Bible (Webster, 1964; Eades, 1980: 11). Often they adopted Western names, styles of dress, and mannerisms (Fadipe, 1970: 326; McIntyre, 1967: 113–14).

Those who found their way homeward "quickly became men of substance and social importance among their people," partly thanks to their newly acquired reading and writing skills (Fadipe, 1970: 49). These repatriated Yoruba slaves, or *Saro*, invited Christian missionaries to settle among them. In 1843, the first white missionary, the Reverend H. Townsend of CMS, arrived in Abeokuta, where "he was received with open arms" (Fadipe, 1970: 49). Townsend arranged for Yorubaland's first printing press and began to publish a newspaper. By 1853 Samuel (Ajayi) Crowther, a Saro who was to become the first African bishop of the Anglican Church and who had accompanied Townsend from Sierra Leone into Yorubaland, had published a Yoruba primer and translated much of the Bible, a catechism, and a hymnbook into Yoruba.

Since Christianity was the door to formal education—and education, it became increasingly apparent, would be the means to economic reward in the new order—the number of Yorubas willing to identify themselves as Christian increased (Ayandele, 1974; Fadipe, 1970: 322; Orubuloye, 1981).[8] English was fast becoming (and would remain) a common language throughout Nigeria. English literacy and numeracy were soon prerequisites to Yoruba employment not only in the advancing political bureaucracy but also in the growing British trade with the interior.

The mission schools took children away from the direct supervision of their families and out of the traditional apprenticeship system (Fadipe, 1970: 315). African sociologists T. Kabwegyere and J. Mbula describe the advent of Christianity thus: "The mission used the drum to call congregations together. The drum sounded the war alarm in African society. The missionary drum sounded a war against African values. . . . We must remember that the Christian message came at the same time as the capitalist message and the conqueror's message" (1979: 27, 30).

Western education thus created a class of relatively privileged, typically Europeanized indigenes whose attitudes and interests were separate from those of the masses (Fadipe, 1970: 322; see also Amin, 1976: 218). Providing personnel for advancing colonial economic and political bureaucracies, this educated class became increasingly removed from the rest of their people. Nevertheless, they were the ones who would organize and lead the nationalistic movement that eventually liberated Nigeria politically.

Resistance and Political Liberation

The late nineteenth century marked the beginnings of organized Yoruba nationalism, largely in response to increasingly apparent racism on the part of the British. Many Saro who had adopted Christian names returned to Yoruba names and openly criticized the Crown (Eades, 1980: 35). By the early twentieth century Frobenius was worried that Lagos blacks were failing increasingly to show whites "proper respect." The escalating situation was hardly trivial, he warned; it had to do with "racial power and racial will" (1913: 38–41).

In 1920 Yoruba professionals and merchants held a conference in Accra, on the Gold Coast. The Accra Conference called for indigenous enfranchisement, greater control over Nigeria's natural resources (viewed by England, according to conference members, as "free property for exploitation by British concessionaires under state protection"), and more equitable treatment of indigenous landholders (Arikpo, 1967: 56–57).

Nigeria's Governor Hugh Clifford defined the Accra resolutions as "farcical" and "a great deal of loose and gaseous talk" (quoted in Arikpo, 1967: 39). More generally, however, Britain's reaction was consternation. In the words of one 1930 colonial memo: "You free them, you give them equitable laws, more or less, and show them a means, by trading, of becoming rich and comfortable and safe, and before you know where you are they want to drive you out imagining that they can govern themselves because one or two have been educated" (quoted in Isichei, 1983: 391). Nevertheless, by the late 1930s, Yorubas were demanding complete autonomy within the British Commonwealth, along with economic opportunities "equal to those enjoyed by foreigners," and an emergent indigenous press summoned Nigerians to "throw off the shackles of imperialism" (quoted in Arikpo, 1967: 59).

Nationalist activism temporarily receded during World War II. But as Nigerians fought in Europe, overseas service broadened their political perspective. The Allies' war rhetoric, extolling parliamentary democracy, stimulated discussion about self-determination. In 1941 Franklin Roosevelt and Winston Churchill signed the Atlantic Charter, and Britain's deputy prime minister stated publicly that Africans were as much entitled to the benefits of the charter as any other peoples. But when challenged by Africans to confirm the statement officially, Churchill was evasive. As a result, Yoruba leaders— among others—demanded independence (Arikpo, 1967: 61).

Nigeria Today

On October 1, 1960, Nigeria gained political independence. Since then it has alternated between civilian and military governments. The initial parliamentary democracy, known as the First Republic, lasted a little over five years. According to Isichei (1983: 468): "The parliamentary experiment was wrecked by two related factors: the politics of ethnicity and the theory of winner-take-all." As Samir Amin (1976: 318) has pointed out, the nation–states of Africa resulted from an "artificial carve-up" of that continent imposed by outsiders and did not arise naturally from any cultural or ideological unity. Ethnic antagonisms that had existed for many centuries had only been exacerbated by colonialism.

Moreover, officials felt greater allegiance to themselves and to their compounds, friends, and ethnic groups than to the country as a whole. Following tradition, Nigeria's new leaders "were expected to be generous, by western standards absurdly generous, to relations, fellow townsmen and constituents" (Isichei, 1983: 468). Patronage, bribery, and embezzlement were real, if not ideal, norms. Hugh H. and Mabel M. Smythe (1960: 132) view this situation as an understandable outcome of Nigeria's colonial history: "The British elite had not been responsible to the masses, except indirectly and in a very special sense; the new [indigenous] elite accepted the same remoteness from the popular will as their natural and proper role."

After all, the officials were drawn from a class already significantly removed from the masses by Western education, language, and attitude. The comments of John G. Patterson and Nanda R. Shrestha about new Third World nations are applicable to Nigeria:

> In the aftermath of independence from colonialism most . . . newly emerging nations failed to uproot colonial social formation or structure and break the chain of economic dependency. With very few exceptions, most of these countries . . . have been ruled by a small minority of domestic elites. These ruling elites . . . have invariably turned to their previous colonial rulers and the United States for development policy guidance and economic and military support, thereby further deepening their dependency. . . . These dominant compradores, despite their nationalistic rhetoric, continue to maintain their dependency linkages with the advanced capitalist nations because their interests are much more closely bound both by economic ties and by political ones to those of the imperialist masters.

On January 15, 1966, a group of young army majors overthrew the First Republic in a bloody coup, which "it seems clear . . . was intended as a radical and nationalist protest against the tribalism and corruption of the politicians" (Isichei, 1983: 471). The resulting military government lasted until October 1, 1979, when Nigerians went to the polls to put in place a second presidential democracy, known as the Second Republic. But for much the same reasons as those that had led to the earlier coup, the Second Republic did not last and was replaced in 1983 by a new military government. Politically aligned with the West, this government has continued to the time of this writing, despite an attempted coup in April 1990. A new constitution was scheduled to take effect by October 1, 1992 ("Nigeria," 1991: 2007).

Demographic Parallels with the Historical Themes

Historically, the general Eurocentric devaluation of the Yoruba meant that Europeans felt free to make whatever use they chose of Yorubaland resources. The extraction of Third World fertility data by First World demographic researchers may be seen as a contemporary counterpart to this exploitation of resources. Furthermore, devaluation has meant the persistent assumption that changes in Third World societies resulting from First World cultural penetration would be unqualifiedly acceptable as evidence of "transition" and "progress" (see Chapter 4). The possibility that science inspired and administered by core nations might be reactive, peripheralizing the cultures in which it operates, is not a major ethical consideration within world-system demography.

The second historical theme is the de- and reconstruction of Yoruba social structure and culture by means of an imposed economy. Exploitation of raw materials, coupled with the marketing of British products in Yorubaland, initiated the deconstruction of the traditional economy. Later, cash crop production, compulsory labor, and taxation in money rather than in kind reconstructed the economy by bringing Nigeria into the world system as peripheral. This de- and reconstruction of Third World societies and cultures continues in world-system demography in that its research questions impose on Yoruba views of reality lessons based on Western assumptions of family and personal values (see Chapter 5).

The third historical theme is that because of sparse European settlement, social change in Nigeria was largely orchestrated from without. Although marines and muskets initiated colonialization, ongoing geographic expansion and control were effected by increasingly centralized bureaucratic surveillance. Similarly, demographic research in the Third World is largely controlled from without by First World actors. Such research rests upon bureaucratic surveillance, the groundwork for which was effectively laid during colonialism. Externally controlled surveillance made use of indigenes as bureaucratic subordinates. During the nineteenth century, traditional leaders in Yorubaland became subordinates in British-controlled political and economic bureaucracies. As time passed, Yorubas educated in Western schools moved into these positions and became a class of Westernized indigenous elites. Western education now is similarly a requirement for employment as a fieldworker in Third World demographic research directed by First World agencies (see Chapter 3).

The fourth theme, indigenous resistance to colonialization and cultural penetration, initially meant sporadic rioting. Resistance later emerged in nationalistic movements, effectively pressing Nigeria toward political independence. Similarly, Third World respondents find ways to resist the cultural penetration inherent in demographic research (see Chapter 6).

Conclusion

The Europeans' invasion of Yorubaland was first effected by military force, thanks largely to their exclusive possession of naval gunnery. As time went on, bureaucratically organized surveillance supplanted explosives, the latter employed only when other means failed. Since relatively few British lived in Yorubaland, given the hostile climate, educated indigenes were gradually trained to provide administrative personnel. Growing Yoruba resistance to invasion, however, resulted in political independence in 1960.

Parallels to this historical legacy can be seen in world-system demography—worldwide, bureaucratically organized, core-controlled demographic research—and are reflected in the Changing African Family–Nigeria projects. As we will see in Chapter 5, de- and reconstruction of Yoruba society and culture involved beliefs and values regarding personal efficacy, the nuclear family, and "reasonable" family size as purposefully controlled. That the research was potentially reactive was not a consideration.

Designed, funded, and administered from outside Yorubaland by First World professionals, CAFN became an exercise in bureaucratic surveillance. Implementing the research depended upon employing Western-educated Yoruba fieldworkers, the precedent for which had been effectively set during colonialism. The following chapter describes the motivation and training of those fieldworkers as they carried world-system demography to the Yoruba masses.

3   The Yoruba
Fieldworkers
Emissaries of
Bureaucratic
Surveillance

By the 1950s, as Nigeria edged toward political independence, several hundred Western social scientists had found their way to British Africa. Perhaps 75 percent of these were English; another 20 percent were American (Lee, 1967: 24). The stage was set for First World cultural imposition to continue, one agent of that imposition being world-system demography.

Like the Westernized, educated indigenes of the colonial period, Yoruba fieldworkers for the CAFN projects were linked to the economy of the new world order. Bureaucratically organized, the CAFN projects were characterized by hierarchical sub- and superordination, specialized training, functional division of labor, and well-defined areas of jurisdiction, supervision, and documentary procedures (Weber, 1958). Like any well-managed, large-scale research enterprise, this bureaucratic organization established internal authority and discipline. Rigorously trained and tightly supervised subordinates became professional experts, emissaries of the core-influenced elites who directed the research.

Put another way, subordinates became socialized, loyal members of a bureaucratically controlled "performance team" (Goffman, 1959). Teams of this sort involve members' collusion to impose or sustain

33

one of many arbitrary (cf. Bourdieu, 1977) and possibly competing definitions of a situation (Goffman, 1959: 80). With regard to world-system demography, one definition to be imposed and maintained is the legitimacy of worldwide scientific surveillance. But there is always the possibility that a team member will perform inappropriately or "give the show away" (Goffman, 1959: 98). To guard against this in Nigeria, CAFN principals fashioned a network of lateral and hierarchical supervision by means of which supervisors acted as field-work team directors.

The principal researchers expended "an unusually high amount of effort and money" (Caldwell and Ware, 1977: 489) in selecting and training the qualified Yorubas who would become members of a vast, bureaucratically organized team of experts. Several hundred Yoruba interviewers, editors, coders, and supervisors—all necessarily bilingual—came to the project with a minimum of four years of secondary education.[1] Many were social science students at the University of Ibadan. A significant percentage came from the ranks of the educated unemployed (Okediji et al., 1976: 136). Once selected, the staff spent several days at project headquarters in the Department of Social Sciences, University of Ibadan. In this scholastic and thereby prestigious setting, subordinates joined the principal researcher elites to form one team of scientific experts and were trained in appropriate team attitudes and behavior.

The Subordinates as Yorubas

The project's indigenous subordinates could be expected to exemplify characteristic Yoruba attitudes and behaviors. To some extent they joined respondents in what Alfred Schutz (1970: 253–54) has called the "paramount reality" of everyday Yoruba life. That is, they engaged with respondents in activities characterized by "the natural attitude" of spontaneity and suspension of doubt. Not only did they share the respondents' first language; they joked, ate, and drank with them. Sometimes interviews more closely approximated everyday Yoruba visiting behavior than formal and objective information-gathering exercises as we know them in the West.

Not infrequently, interviewers evidenced the traditional Yoruba understanding of reasonable family size. In the following, for instance, an interviewer refers to a respondent's desire for eight children as illustrating "the value of having a few":

> He wishes his children to be six, at present he has five. The income of his wife and . . . his is poor. They do not want to have many children they would be unable to cater for. The family wishes to do family planning. He told me that if they are fortunate to become rich in the future, they would have at least two more to make eight. . . . From my own point of view . . . he reaches the value of having a few children. (CAFN2-fn: 1918)

Occasionally, a fieldworker would even temporarily abandon expert team training to form a short-lived alliance with a respondent. One interviewer, describing a man with only one child, closed with the sentence, "I pray that may God Almighty hear his prayer and provide him more children. Amen" (CAFN2-fn: 1102). In another case an interviewer omitted sensitive questions when a respondent became distraught:

> The woman is very unhappy. . . . I thought she was joking when she told me she has no issue. When I refused to believe, a cousin of hers in the house testified to the fact that all her children died in their infant age. She even started to weep, but as a Yoruba man I tried to comfort her with some wits [jokes] until I finished the interview. I avoided some questions that might precipitate her gloomy feelings. (CAFN2-fn: 1675)

Job Performance

For the most part, however, subordinates performed as expected on behalf of the team. For instance, most fieldworkers were very willing to amplify data for superiors. Interviewers had access to information neither directly required of nor offered by the respondent, and some were particularly adept at observation:

> A lot of things [were] observed from the woman's activities during the course of the interview. I was able to detect out that

apart from the normal occupation of weaving, the woman still engage[s] herself in making *gari* [cassava flour] for sale.

Again, I was able to observe how the woman attempted to feed her children because it was [the] dinner period. Every child was given enough food to eat, and they ate separately. I could also observe that the husband engage[s] in part-time farming to supplement his earnings from blacksmithing, because some of his children arrived from farm with maize and yams just at the period the interview was going on.

It was clear from my observation that the senior wife did not eat the same kind of food with the junior wife, but this had nothing to do with their relationships, which appeared to be very cordial.

From all indications, it appears as if the woman is living happily in the family together with her children and the children of the senior wife. (CAFN2-fn: 0640)

In some cases interviewers related respondents' goals, concerns, or anxieties. About a male petty trader and farm worker who had four children and wanted more, experts read, "He wishes to become a very rich man in the future" (CAFN2-fn: 1362). Another respondent's anxiety over unemployment since his divorce, one interviewer volunteered in a final note, "seems to have affected all the responses given" (CAFN2-fn: 0024).

Most often, CAFN2 final notes focused directly on the fertility matters with which the research was concerned: "On the whole the man is ready to produce as many children as his seeds can produce" (CAFN2-fn: 1371); "She has no idea about contraceptives except abstinence" (CAFN2-fn: 0294). And again:

This is a respondent with definite opinions of her own. . . . One striking fact about her is that she does not see any reason for family planning. (CAFN2-fn: 1192)

On occasion, these final notes evidenced a fieldworker's attitudinal affiliation with the First World. "I am much impressed by the man," wrote one interviewer, "*despite* the fact that he develops much interest in having as many children as the number of twenty" (CAFN2-fn: 1352; emphasis added); "She sounds to be highly intelligent and knows the bad effect of having many children" (CAFN2-fn: 1677). And again:

Despite her low level of education, she seems to be speaking for those who have learned about and accepted the value of small family size.

She finds the questions interesting. She responds well to them with little or no embarrassment.

It is wonderful that Religion has no influence on her thought. (CAFN2-fn: 2178)

Western Education and Subordinates' Loyalty

It was their education that had prepared these Yoruba subordinates to be loyal CAFN employees. For one thing, as Western-educated indigenes, they typically viewed rural, uneducated Yorubas as "entirely superstitious" persons (CAFN2-fn: 0277), "pagans" (CAFN2-dr: p. 21), or the "real natives" (CAFN1-br: p. 21). Formal education has since colonization been a principal agent in socializing the less powerful to the dominant world view (Bourdieu, 1977). Alex Inkeles and David H. Smith's (1974) empirical study of the process whereby Third World people move from "traditional" to "modern personalities" (that is, become open to new experience and information, accept social change, and have a sense of efficacy) concluded that the Western school was causally significant as "a context for modernity."

CAFN subordinate staff, then, were not simply embodied locations of Yoruba everyday life or traditional culture. Rather, the prospective fieldworker approximated Schutz's "well-informed citizen" when hired; he or she had access to "a number of frames of reference" (1970: 242). Subordinates consequently identified not only with traditional or everyday Yoruba life but also with Western values, among them the merit of bureaucratically organized social structure. Randall Collins (1979) has pointed out that organizations increasingly use formal educational credentials for the "cultural selection" of employees. More important than assuring specific job skills, this "credential system" indicates a prospective employee's socialization to appropriate attitudes. With regard to CAFN, the appropriate attitudes promised by the credential system were willingness to identify with the research project and belief in—or at least acceptance of—its goals and means.

Moreover, Western schools are training grounds for the acceptance of and participation in bureaucratic surveillance. Since the eighteenth century, surveillance has been integral to disciplinary institutions such as the military, the factory, and the elementary school (Foucault, 1975: 138–39). In fact, with advancing modernity, schools were architecturally and social-structurally designed to serve supervisory, or surveillance, requirements (Foucault, 1975: 138–43). One might therefore expect that staff, who had experienced and practiced compliance in the surveillance systems of Western schools, would be willing to accept the bureaucratic discipline of CAFN supervisors and directors.

Team Coalescence and Subordinates' Loyalty

A related reason that subordinates generally proved loyal to the expert team was the remarkable ability of the directors to catalyze team coalescence. One method was to use a large, informal discussion meeting as "a kind of day-to-day research steering group" (Okediji et al., 1976: 135). Principal researchers were present at such gatherings, along with field supervisors, prospective editors and coders, and some interviewers. The principal researchers have described these "most successful" meetings:

> This group began to form as night fell and continued in vigorous session until near midnight each day for almost a year. The membership was not completely constant but there was a solid nucleus consisting of the principals and most of those who became the backbone of the supervisory, editing, and coding staff. It was overwhelmingly Yoruba in composition and was drawn from a surprising range of walks of life, especially as there were always a few people attending who were not strictly members of the team but who were interested in aspects of their own society. They ranged

from chiefs to journalists, artists, and actors, as well as people from other social science research teams. Certainly many stayed on to enjoy the food and drink, but discussion raged and the subject was always the analysis of the day's experience and the revised plans for the morrow (Okediji et al., 1976: 135).

As Goffman has pointed out, "the very fact that an important effect is not striven for tends to set the tone for interaction, leading those who find themselves there to act as if they were on familiar terms with one another in all matters" (1959: 125–26). The fluid membership, camaraderie and easy talk of the CAFN late-night sessions helped effect elite-subordinate team cohesion.

The principal cause of subordinates' loyalty, however, was most likely economic. Many had been unemployed before joining the CAFN staff and were presumably grateful for professional work of the kind toward which they had been schooled. As Weber (1968, vol. 3: 968) has pointed out, a person's cooperation (or at least compliance) is best achieved by "an assured salary connected with the opportunity of a career." Put another way, bureaucratically organized surveillance, as exemplified in the CAFN projects, became "linked from the inside to the economy and to the aims of the mechanism in which it was practised" (Foucault, 1975: 176).

The Bureaucratic Supervision Network

Once formed, the scientific team was carefully managed and controlled. Among other things, subordinates were trained to recognize and respect the hierarchy of status and roles characteristic of bureaucracy. Staff used appropriate titles ("Dr.," "Professor," "Mr." or "Mrs.") when referring to superiors. Use of such titles reminded interviewers of their legitimately subordinate status within the organization, rendering them willing to defer to superiors in the impersonal public sphere while simultaneously preserving personal or private self-respect. This situation facilitated bureaucratic supervision and thereby, in Weber's terms (1968, vol. 3: 968), "the official's integration into the given functional conditions of the disciplined mechanism"; by means of "taut discipline and control," coupled with "prestige

sentiments of the status group," subordinates were effectively socialized to the paradigm of world-system demography and hence to belief
in the legitimacy of scientific surveillance.

Foucault has discussed bureaucratic surveillance as a method for
social control that is "organized as a . . . network of relations from
top to bottom, but also to a certain extent from bottom to top and
laterally; this network 'holds' the whole together and traverses it
in its entirety with effects of power that derive from one another:
supervisors, perpetually supervised" (1975: 176–77). In just such an
intricate supervision network, CAFN principal researchers managed
not only interviewers, but field supervisors, editors, and coders (who
prepared the collected data for computer entry). Field supervisors
reported on interviewers. In evaluating completed questionnaires,
editors and coders oversaw the work of field supervisors and interviewers. This interwoven hierarchy has been described in detail by
the principal researchers:

> The philosophy of the fieldwork was essentially a near saturation
> degree of supervision and checking. One supervisor or checker was
> employed for every two interviewers. All sample areas or houses
> were independently checked both to make sure that they had been
> visited and to ascertain that all residents had been listed and eli-
> gible respondents identified. . . .
>
> Supervisors and office editors were chosen from among inter-
> viewers and had to keep up some experience in interviewing.
> Supervisors were frequently rotated so that they would not form
> friendships with interviewers, which could lead to emotional pres-
> sure to accept shoddy or incomplete work. They left detailed
> diaries, which were used by the principals for field checks. There
> is no substitute for such checks in keeping up standards and en-
> thusiasm in fieldwork—visibility is important.
>
> Office editors and coders had all been interviewers and were
> often rotated back into interviewing. Each interviewer was de-
> briefed by an editor for almost as long as interviews took in the
> field. First, the interviewer was expected to describe the respon-
> dent in general so as to place everything in perspective. Then the

interview was gone through in detail and each response was discussed in order to pick up errors in coding and incomplete statements as well as evidence of hurried or slapdash interviews where rapport with the respondent appeared to be inadequate. Wherever there were problems—and with this degree of thoroughness there were problems in quite a high proportion of interviews— the interviewer, together with a supervisor, returned to see the respondent. . . .

All coding was gone through twice by different coders and all referrals for decisions were made to the principal investigators. Each schedule identified the interviewer, supervisor, and editor and all questionable responses were referred back to them (Okediji et al., 1976: 135–36).

The directors noted that although detailed in this way the system sounds authoritarian, in fact a "family atmosphere was created" as the discussion groups described above "proceeded convivially far into the night" (Okediji et al., 1976: 136).

The Supervisory Role of the Team Directors

Within this atmosphere, principal researchers hired and promoted staff; developed interviewer's and editor's manuals (Appendix B, #4, 16, 33); and dispensed various memos with regard to sampling (Appendix B, #8, 24, 25), editing (Appendix B, #5, 16, 20, 23, 31, 34), and coding (Appendix B, #7, 13, 22, 36–38). Meanwhile, interviewers and field supervisors were required to submit daily or weekly written progress reports on specific forms designed for the purpose (Appendix B, #17, 18, 21, 28, 29, 39).[2]

Principal researchers periodically extended their supervisory roles to the field by visiting various research centers, sometimes unannounced (CAFN2-dr: pp. 3, 4, 15). Field Director Helen Ware often made such visits. The Caldwells might also appear at research sites; CAFN2 Daily Reports relate that "Professor J. C. Caldwell and Mrs. Pat Caldwell" visited the research center of Odogbolu and Isiwo on July 8, 1973, for example. During that visit, "progress so far made was commended . . ." (CAFN2-dr: p. 3). Nine days later the Caldwells visited the center again, lunching with interviewers, reviewing completed questionnaires, and urging them "to find all people already interviewed, to complete additional questions" (CAFN2-dr: p. 4). More commonly, however, Yoruba supervisors visited interviewers in the field.

Yoruba Subordinates as Fieldwork Supervisors

The supervision network was both hierarchical and lateral with "supervisors perpetually supervised," to repeat Foucault's words (1975: 176). A typical CAFN2 entry: "The supervisor later came and found the work which we had done to be satisfactory" (CAFN2-dr: p. 23). In an entry for July 12, 1973, a supervisor reported from Igede-Ekiti:

> I visited the Station between 12 noon and 2 P.M. and found that the interviewers have worked very hard. I am much impressed by performances. They are hard-working people. (CAFN2-dr: p. 15)

From Aramoko-Ekiti:

> The Supervisor, Mr. I. Orubuloye, visited us. "I visited the Station on the 9th July; the interviewers were working very hard." (CAFN2-dr: p. 7)

And from Ikun-Igogo a report headed "First Supervision":

> The station was visited by me today (11th July, 1973). Five questionnaires were edited. I am very much impressed about the performances of the interviewers—the sampling done before my arrival was very good and the questionnaires completed were very good. (CAFN2-dr: p. 32)

On July 16, 1973, a fieldworker recorded the results of a supervisor's visit to Ilawe-Ekiti:

> The Supervisor for our area came on this day. He supervised our work. We asked more about the areas of the work which we did not understand. . . . He looked at our sketch map for Ilawe and he commended our efforts. . . . He made a suggestion

that we should go back to the individual respondents we have already done to enquire about their religion. We did according to instruction. (CAFN2-dr: p. 12)

Field supervisors might team up with interviewers when necessary to help with village mapping (see Chapter 4) or to attempt to persuade difficult respondents to cooperate. In some cases supervisors and interviewers revisited respondents together in order to discuss inconsistent answers (Caldwell and Ware, 1977: 489). When not visited in person, interviewers might report to project headquarters by telephone. On one such occasion Dr. Ware impressed upon an interviewer the need to recontact respondents in order to remedy unsatisfactory questionnaires (CAFN2-dr: p. 4).

Ongoing Training

This operation of the supervision network coincided with ongoing training for subordinates at all levels, often through memos. From one memo, for example, used in both CAFN2 and CAFN3, staff learned the meaning of open-ended coding:

There are some cases in which those asking the questions may not know in advance what the answers are going to be, or may in any case wish to allow as much freedom as possible in the answers. In these cases no codes are provided [on the questionnaire] for the interviewer to use at the time of the interview, and the coding is done later in the office by coders reading the answers given. Such coding is called open-ended coding because the original questions were open-ended, i.e., they allowed the respondent to give any answer at all and were not fixed choice questions such as "Have you ever used an I.U.D.?"—which required the answer Yes or No. (Appendix B, #15)

The supervision network also permitted bureaucratic subordinates to be drilled in responsible, efficient work habits, a requirement for bureaucratically organized employees in general. For instance, the CAFN1 Interviewer's Manual (Appendix B, #4) concludes with a grading system:

You will be given a score of points for each day's interviewing.
For each Part A—1 point
For each Part B—2 points
(i.e. for a whole questionnaire 3 points). At the end of each day
you will get a score for how well the questionnaires are filled in.
Very well = 2;   Well = 1;   Fair = 0
Over the week you should average 10 points per day—that is
you should score 60 points per week. Scores of less than 50 will
have to be explained. (Though interviewing in outer areas where
there are very few or no houses will be an explanation).

And the CAFN3 Interviewer's Manual (Appendix B, #33) advised subordinates who had to return to a house at night for an interview to
say so in their daily reports so that the situation could be taken into
account by those evaluating their performance. "What we will not
accept is people who consistently turn in report sheets showing very
little work and no adequate explanation."

This tight supervision network could be established and kept in
place because subordinates' salaries and continued employment depended upon their cooperation within it. From the CAFN3 interviewer's manual:

If by the 25th June you have not been out with a supervisor
you should come into the office and ask for one to go with you.
This is in your own interest as people whose work has not been
checked will not be paid.

And from a memo by Pat Caldwell marked "IMPORTANT":

Unless all interviewers have had satisfactory check with supervisors regarding no. of children living and dead and also question 13 checked out we will not keep them on after Wednesday.

As a result, some interviewers used CAFN2 Daily Reports and
CAFN2 or CAFN3 Final Notes to support and explain their work
performance.[3] From the villages of Odogbolu and Isiwo, for example,
fieldworkers asserted that "care was taken" in mapping (CAFN2-dr:
p. 2),[4] and from Igogo-Ekiti that upon arriving there they "quickly

settled down" to work (CAFN2-dr: p. 21). Often, explanations accounted for loss of time in the field. For example, subordinates reported from Ado-Ekiti that, "it took us many hours to finish because [the majority of respondents] are sellers [and thus] the interviews were always off and on" (CAFN2-dr: p. 27). Similarly, Owo fieldworkers made a point of explaining loss of time:

It should be noted that in fact we had to consult more than five houses a day, because of those who actually refused or promised that we should come back the next day if they grew tired. This was what wasted the time.   (CAFN2-dr: p. 9)

I wasted much time with this woman. There were many situations I was left while she went in to cook or take something; I was all the while patient. She told me that she was feeling sleepy and that I should come the second day. . . . I came the second day.   (CAFN2-fn: 1697)

Not surprisingly, fieldworkers came to prefer subjects who wasted little time; an especially "good" respondent was one who "never hesitates at all" (CAFN2-fn: 1221). "Good" respondents made interviewers "really happy" (CAFN1-fn: 1107) or "impressed" them (CAFN1-fn: 1137, 1380, 1389, 2167). Fieldworkers often described compliant subjects as "enlightened" (CAFN2-fn: 2174) or "responsible" (CAFN3-sr: 0382; see Appendix B, #51), "wise" or "intelligent." For example,

This man was very wise in giving me answers to the questions. He took patience and explained every detail of the answers to me.   (CAFN2-fn: 1105)

This particular woman answered my questions very intelligently. She welcomed me heartily and never waste[d] my time on giv[ing] her long explanations. Her answers were very short and to the point.   (CAFN2-fn: 1134)

I found the respondent very interesting to deal with and he tried to shelf his embarrassment and view the questions critically before answering them. He is very intelligent.   (CAFN2 fn: 1723)

Conversely, refusal to comply was often attributed to ignorance: "They were very ignorant, and despite all my explanations, they still ran away" (CAFN1-fn: 1101).

In their expressed concerns about the efficient use of time as a scarce resource, interviewers exemplified the expert world view as opposed to the daily-life perspective of Yorubas, in which time is viewed as ongoing and virtually limitless. As both Yorubas and experts, the CAFN subordinates moved effectively between the two worlds of world-system demography and everyday Yoruba life. In so doing, they extended bureaucratic surveillance in Yorubaland.

Conclusion

One ongoing historical theme with which the Changing African Family–Nigeria projects were in keeping was the fact that surveillance was controlled from without by First World actors who employed Western-educated indigenes as subordinates. The school system in Nigeria had produced educated Yorubas, prospective personnel suitable for CAFN employment. As Yorubas, they spoke the language and otherwise identified with and took part in everyday Yoruba life. But they spoke English (the language of the colonizers and, later, the demographers) as well. Moreover, their schooling had familiarized them with and rendered them accepting of bureaucratic administration and surveillance.

As members of a bureaucratically organized (that is, hierarchically ordered and rigorously supervised) opportunity structure, Yoruba staff found themselves integrated "into the functional conditions of [that] mechanism" (Weber, 1968, vol. 3: 968). Together with elites, these subordinates made up a scientific team of experts. The definition of the situation which the team sought to impose and maintain embodied the right to invade subjects' privacy—with little or no regard to issues of cultural imposition—in order to gather demographic information. How did they go about gaining entrance into the lives and opinions of their subjects?

4   Gaining Entrance

An army of indigenous fieldworkers—subordinates in the CAFN bureaucracy—moved between world-system demography and everyday Yoruba life. They carried questionnaires to the field, then relayed data back to directors for analysis. An early report from a CAFN1 interviewer illustrates various aspects of the process of gaining entrance into their subjects' lives:

> My first day at block 40 which is in the Yemetu Adeoyo area was very encouraging to me. The first house I went into was the very best. The people there were very nice and they seemed very eager to answer my questions and they were also ready with lots of questions for me to answer.
>
> The other houses did not give me the same welcome. Some even went as far as to slam the door in my face. But I did get most of them to talk to me. (CAFN1-br: p. 12).

This report raises several points developed in this chapter. First, the fact that the fieldworker could refer to a "block 40" in Ibadan was due to surveillance carried out as part of the overall Changing African Family–Nigeria project. Second, though most subjects were eventually compliant, many were initially reticent, and some never

47

did cooperate. Third, respondents who accepted the questioning experience eagerly were likely to define it as an everyday-life dialogue—asking questions in their turn—rather than a scientific interview. Overall, as we shall see, gaining entrance—an invasion of subjects' privacy—could prove troublesome.

"Block 40" and Surveillance

The CAFN research design involved random sampling of Yorubas in Nigeria's western region. Random sampling requires detailed geographic information, but considerable portions of Lagos and other states in the region had never been accurately surveyed. In Ibadan, for example,

> lack of housing lists, the absence of a house numbering system, the huge heterogeneous street blocks (the bigger ones containing tens of thousands of people because of the relatively small number of streets in the inner city), and the tendency in the traditional core area for houses to be built against each other or be connected by earth walls meant that simple listing with random selection was practically impossible. (Okediji et al., 1976: 135)

Hence, at the onset of CAFN, scientists devoted considerable attention to geographic surveillance. Fieldworkers visited virtually every residence in Ibadan and listed each household member. As the CAFN1 Interviewer's Manual emphasized, "Every woman who sleeps in [the fieldworker's] area at night is to be counted—whether she sleeps in her shop, under some stairs, in her stall, in a tiny hut, in the servants' quarters, or wherever else" (Appendix B, #4).

For CAFN2, entire villages and "cake slice"–shaped segments of towns were carefully mapped—by hand—for the first time ever (Okediji et al., 1976: 135); Map 3 is an example. CAFN2 Daily Reports typically begin with subordinates' descriptions of "important" mapping activities. While this surveillance was a necessary sampling prerequisite, project directors also emphasized that an interviewer was to be able to relocate each subject in order to check responses that were incomplete or seemed inaccurate. Thus, for the first time in history, many Yorubas fell under the eye of bureaucratic surveillance,

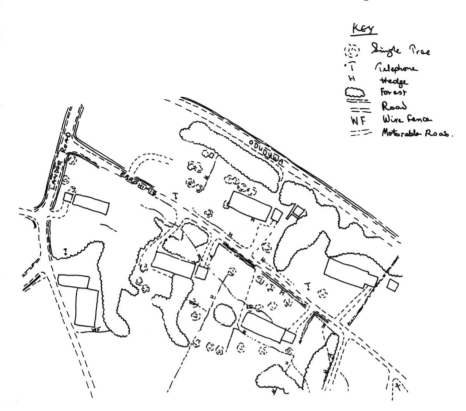

Map 3. CAFN2 Fieldworker's Hand-drawn Map of Town Segment

the acuity of which they had not previously known. Illustrating a condition of advancing modernity, they became, to use Schutz's words, "potentially subject to everybody's remote control" (1970: 239).

Once the subjects' locations had been geographically surveyed, fieldworkers turned their attention to gaining compliance, a process that involved knowing how and when to use the cultural capital of both the indigenous and the penetrating culture.

Utilizing Cultural Capital from Two Worlds

Not only for methodological issues of validity and reliability but also to facilitate the process of gaining entrance, considerable effort went into creating a questionnaire that would not strike a respondent as foreign:

> Actors in folk theater, skilled in getting a simple message over to all, and interviewers who had shown both an interest and an ability in communicating with other sections of the society were employed in producing questionnaires that were unmistakably Yoruba and that were couched in traditional proverbial expressions and ways of looking at things. (Okediji et al., 1976: 134)

Questions were first constructed in Yoruba, then translated to English, rather than vice versa. The interviewers, unlike not only the majority of respondents but also the principal researchers, spoke both English and Yoruba. Greeting and conversing with respondents in their traditional language was a major step in gaining entrance (Okediji et al., 1976: 134).[1] In addition, the researchers made a conscious attempt "to fit in with Yoruba codes of manners by first avoiding direct questions which were held to be ill-mannered" (Caldwell and Ware, 1977: 489). Participant knowledge of Yoruba manners and customs was cultural capital in the hands of entrance-gaining fieldworkers.

"I told him that we had been to the palace to see the king"

For one thing, because they were themselves Yoruba, fieldworkers could feel comfortable contacting Yoruba influence resources (traditional village, town, or neighborhood leaders), appealing to them as members of the same ethnic group. In Ishua, CAFN2 interviewers went initially "to the Oba's palace to introduce ourselves to him. We told him the object of our mission and he promised to help us whenever we need his assistance" (CAFN2-dr: p. 23). Likewise, in Igogo-Editi the team went first to the king, or Oba, who gave them a place to stay during their visit (CAFN2-dr: p. 20). And interviewers met first with the Oba of Odogbolu and Isiwo ("an intelligent man of about 60 years" and "a life member of Lagos Tennis Club"), who promised to send his bellman out to request village cooperation (CAFN2-dr: p. 2).

The usefulness of such contacts is apparent in an Iwo interviewer's report of having successfully appealed to traditional authority:

This is the first man I interviewed in Iwo. He is not ready to answer at first but when I told him that we had been to the palace to see the king and that he is the one who authorized us, . . . he agreed to answer my questions. (CAFN2-fn: 1173)

The Yoruba fieldworkers' experiential understanding of their subjects' habits and beliefs was also useful. For example, one supervisor knew and could explain that to make the work easier it is best to find an elderly woman who is willing to call the other women out, because they are used to obeying elderly people (CAFN1-br: p. 26). Another fieldworker, relying on the traditional concept of reincarnation, suggested:

The best way to ask questions on number of deaths is to ask "how many of her children have returned to heaven" and then say in the process that God will return to her those in heaven and keep those on earth. (CAFN2-fn: 1197)

Then too, interviewers knew just how to "pet," "plead with," "beg," or "maneuver" difficult respondents, often "convincing them with patience and persuasion" (CAFN2-fn: 0425, 0461, 0583, 0641, 0605). Occasionally, persuasion involved paying or promising to pay respondents: "Sometimes they ask for some types of presents, . . . and each time I say we are going to distribute them another time" (CAFN1-br: p.110). At least one reluctant subject fared better; she was presented not only with "much persuasion" but also a "gift of 20K" (CAFN2-fn: 0518).

"The bearer of this card is an official interviewer"

At the same time, fieldworkers had access to and made use of First World cultural capital. Even as the mission was initially explained to subjects, it was apparent that the interviewers (armed as they were with interview schedules and pencils) could read, write, and speak English—prestige-laden abilities throughout Yorubaland, even among the uneducated. In addition, each interviewer carried a pair of Western prestige symbols: an identification card and a letter, both printed in English (see Appendix B, #11). These helped to establish a fieldworker's official importance and professional expertise, thereby legitimating entry.[2] The identification card, designed to bear the interviewer's signature, appeared as follows:

The bearer of this card

_____

is an official interviewer
of the Sociology Department of
the University of Ibadan
and is bound to complete
confidentiality.

The accompanying letter also introduced its owner as "an authorized interviewer" affiliated with the Sociology Department of the University of Ibadan and explained that the university was "undertaking a major study of the Nigerian family," a study "of importance." Therefore, the letter continued, "we ask you to collaborate and to urge all other people to do the same." Signed "J. C. Caldwell and F. O. Okediji, Research Directors," the letter assured that all information obtained would be "absolutely anonymous and confidential."

Western church and school personnel also facilitated gaining entrance. In Odogbolu and Isiwo, for example, the interview team met first with a teacher at St. Paul's School. He became "the source of information and arrangements that facilitated our acceptance by the Odogbolu people" (CAFN2-dr: p. 2). A few days later, fieldworkers joined in the morning service at St. Paul's Church, where "the Rev. made our visit to the town known to the congregation" (CAFN2-dr: p. 3). In Owo, interviewers sent messages

to the Headmasters of the schools to ask them to inform their schoolchildren, so that the news might easily spread to their parents to please answer the questions with honor. (CAFN2-dr: p. 9)

Fieldworkers in Ilawe-Ekiti spent their second day going "round to the churches to educate the masses/congregations about our intentions." The next day they "visited schools to educate the teachers about our mission to the town and asked them to inform their parents of the project" (CAFN2-dr: p. 10). Upon arrival at Ikun-Ekiti, interviewers visited pastors to ask that they announce the project to their congregations (CAFN2-dr: p. 32). Occasionally, students too helped fieldworkers to gain entrance. In one section of Ilawe-Ekiti, for example,

> we were fortunate to meet some students who explained our mission to the people with conviction. [Hence] in the houses we visited we enjoyed the maximum cooperation of the respondents. (CAFN2-dr: p. 12)

School and church personnel not only introduced interviewers to the local inhabitants and requested cooperation; they also provided food and accommodation in remote towns and villages. Interviewers were put up at Mayflower School in Odogbolu, for example, after having called at Federal Government College where "the Vice Principal was there to welcome us. He gave useful advice and was very enthusiastic" (CAFN2-dr: pp. 1, 6).

Equipped with cultural capital designed to appeal either to subjects who had (or were impressed by) Western education or to those with more traditional views, fieldworkers employed both kinds— with mixed results. On the second day in Aramoko-Ekiti, for instance, interviewers went to Western churches to request village cooperation, and two days later they visited the traditional "head chief and subchiefs," who promised their "full cooperation" (CAFN2-dr: p. 7). A week later, frustrated by poor compliance throughout the village, the team revisited the churches, again explaining the project and adding that "we are students and nothing more" (CAFN2-dr: p. 8).

A significant proportion of subjects were friendly and "behaved well." Fieldworkers consistently attributed a subject's ability and willingness to cooperate to literacy or education: "The respondent is a literate; she responded well" (CAFN1-fn: 1243); "I did not have any problem in interviewing the woman, since she is educated" (CAFN3-fn: 0109). Those who already favored family planning or purposefully limited families were also likely to be cooperative:

The man was extremely interested in the questions, since according to him he is very interested in family planning. . . . He wants to take part in [a] family planning programme, but unfortunately knows very little about how to control births. (CAFN2-fn: 1172)

"Some of these people are just terrible"

As a group, CAFN3 subjects (persons who said they had purposefully limited their offspring to no more than five live births) were more compliant than either CAFN1 or CAFN2 subjects, the majority of whom initially resisted questioning. Some of the earlier respondents were apparently pleased with the outsiders' attention. As one fieldworker put it, "Gathering from a few women's speech and actions, they are quite appreciative of the fact that someone could get as far as their area." Nevertheless, this same fieldworker continued, "a certain number bluntly refused to understand no matter how much petting or begging" (CAFN1-br: p. 37). "I wouldn't say my work or encounters with people is very easy," wrote a CAFN1 interviewer from Ibadan, "because in about 3 houses they were very aggressive" (CAFN1-br: p. 10). About the people in Ibadan's block 24 a fieldworker reported that "a few of them were very rough; they failed to answer me, and two of them abused me that I was disturbing them and that I should not turn up again" (CAFN1-br: p. 6). At least one interviewer was apparently threatened: "They said that if I go on asking . . . such questions I will soon get an insult in their area" (CAFN1-br: p. 9).

In the villages of Igede-Ekiti and Akungba, "one great problem was persuading the people to give answers," despite the fact that interviewers had met with each Oba, who "gave the best help he could offer us" (CAFN2-dr: pp. 14, 15–16). And in Ogogo-Ekiti, although interviewers "made sure our mission was lucidly explained to the people in the churches, . . . many people did not receive us in their houses" (CAFN2-dr: p. 20).

Some respondents "ran away from home just because of the interview" (CAFN2-fn: 1101). Others shouted at the fieldworker "and even went to the extent of driving me out of their houses" (CAFN1-br: p. 21). At least one subject, an old man, "refused totally to answer the questionnaire—claiming that he is too old to understand any of the questions" (CAFN2-fn: 1144). One woman who turned her interviewer out of the house "insulted me to go ask my mother at home how many children she had" (CAFN2-fn: 1131). In another house, three women "only mocked" the fieldworker, refusing to answer (CAFN2-fn: 1126). As a supervisor appraised her situation: "Some of these people are just terrible" (CAFN1-br: p. 20).

Sources of Difficulty

The fieldworkers' difficulties had several causes. Various subjects defined the interview sessions as too long, unfamiliar, frightening, or contrary to family and personal privacy values.

"She complained about the time spent on the questions"

Interview schedules began with a paragraph to be read to respondents by the interviewer. Designed to enlist cooperation, it assured subjects, among other things, that the inquiry would not take long. For example, to CAFN1 subjects the fieldworkers read an introductory paragraph requesting "a very little" of their time to answer questions that "will take only a few minutes." In fact, the interviews took much more time—up to five hours in some cases. As a result, many respondents found the questions "too many and repetitive" or "monotonous" or unduly "long" (CAFN2-fn: 0067, 1106, 1220, 1602, 1611) and insisted that they had "no time for such a thing" (CAFN2-fn: 1118). The interview team in Owo found the people

> very difficult to trap down because of the length of time taken to interview them. By the time we get to the middle of a single questionnaire, they start getting bored and excusing themselves. (CAFN2-dr: p. 9)

It takes African sociologists to remind us that villagers are "busy people trying to make ends meet. Their work schedule does not allow for a routine of tea breaks, lunch breaks, etc." (Kabwegyere and Mbula, 1979: 21). Nor was it only the village farmers who were busy. One teacher was "very busy" because "his students had just finished their examinations" and there were papers to correct; his interview took "three half-days, some hours in each day" (CAFN2-fn: 1172). (Meanwhile, "in between," the interviewer questioned "others in the house.")

"She demanded what would be the compensation
for this brain-tasking questionnaire"

A second reason that enlisting compliance proved troublesome was that some subjects had difficulty defining the interview situation; it was different from and foreign to their everyday experience, and they wanted to know what good it would do them. For instance, the CAFN1 introductory paragraph described the research as "an investigation of what people want in their lives and how important their families are." This vague statement of purpose suggested an interest in ultimately helping subjects to realize their personal or family goals; indeed, fieldworkers had been trained to emphasize that the research would yield benefits for respondents. As one reported:

On getting to this house I met a pregnant woman to whom I introduced myself. She questioned me, saying, "What have I got to do with all that you are asking me?" I went further to tell her of the benefit my work would be if she happened to answer my questions. (CAFNI-br: p. 2)

The principal researchers had fashioned this approach as a tool for gaining entrance, but some subjects expected benefits to be tangible, immediate, and personal:

She demands from me what we are going to give them to compensate them for their time taken. I assure her that she should be happy that she has the opportunity of speaking out her opinion. (CAFN2-fn: 1295)

She also demanded like many of the respondents what would be the compensation for this brain-tasking questionnaire, but I

tried to enlighten her about the essence of the project and she
left happily.   (CAFN2-fn: 2190)

One woman of over 40 years of age said that I should give her
some *naira* [Nigerian currency] before answering my questions,
because in the early fifties when the government first brought
radio they took down their voices and traditional songs and gave
them money. I had to explain that there was no profit in it for us;
we were only doing research so that the government and white
men would be able to help all Yoruba women.   (CAFN1-br: p. 24)

For a few subjects, to whom scientific surveys were apparently not
an entirely new experience, promises of benefit sparked old angers:

The woman in the first house refused to be interviewed because she said people have been coming for this type of interview but that nothing has been done about it. I explained that
she shouldn't expect immediate effect, but she declined, saying she has the information but is not prepared to give it.
(CAFN1-br: p. 32)

This respondent was difficult to interview. She was very much
against the idea of people coming to ask questions about one's
life and after telling them your problems they do nothing to help
ease the situation.   (CAFN2-fn: 2182)

*"They asked whether the police
are coming to arrest them"*

Then too, some subjects were afraid to participate, even though
interviewers stressed confidentiality to enlist compliance:

I made them realise that everything I was asking them was confidential and cannot be traced back. I told them that many of
my type were interviewing in the same way, and did not ask the
name of house or address, we only need to know the way every
Nigerian woman planned her family.   (CAFN1-br: p. 2)

But scientific confidentiality could be misunderstood. In one instance, when a supervisor returned to an interview site with the original fieldworker in order to check some inconsistent answers, the villagers "grew annoyed" because they had been told that what they said was confidential, yet "we are coming back to them in two's" (CAFN1-br: p. 33).

Others tended to associate fieldworkers with whatever bureaucratic apparatus they did know. Some thought they were taking a census. In another case, an interviewer reported: "After I had finished with some [respondents], they asked whether the police [were] coming to arrest them" (CAFN1-br: p. 19). In three CAFN1 block reports, interviewers said subjects took them for family planning workers[3] and were consequently hostile:

Anytime I entered the area I was called "Family Planner." I found things difficult for the first two days. They told me they haven't got time for me, but after more explanation they have recognized me in that area and I have found things easier. (CAFN1-br: p. 13)

The task was very difficult for me on the first day because people thought that I was from the Family Planning Centre at Adeoyo. It took some hours to convince them, and some did not even listen to me. (CAFN1-br: p. 17)

Moreover, having minimal familiarity with bureaucratically organized secondary relationships, some subjects were fearful of speaking alone with an interviewer:

The woman was not cooperative at all, and it took me quite a long time to extract words from her. . . . She even left me in the house [and] went out to call others because she was afraid. (CAFN2-fn: 2191)

"Women who were already visited came to intrude"

Indeed, the scientists' requirement that subjects be questioned individually, or separate from other family members, was another reason for respondent reticence. In the properly executed interview, "answers were not influenced by any outsider" (CAFN2-fn: 0301), but subjects were frequently uncooperative about this: "Some of the women who were already visited came to intrude so I have to wait longer to get them out of the questions" (CAFN2-fn: 2195).

A CAFN1 interviewer reported that "women in two of these houses refused answering the questions, saying that their husbands should not hear of this" (CAFN1-br: p. 20). Another reported:

My first few days there were not very productive, the people were always dodging me. Some asked me to wait for the male members of their house to come back from work. I told them that my interview had nothing to do with men, but they wouldn't co-operate. (CAFNI-br: p. 23)

Similarly, for a CAFN2 fieldworker, one woman "was not cooperative at all. . . . Before she could answer me, she called all her in-laws to come and see me. I spent several hours in interviewing her" (CAFN2-fn: 1431). Another subject said that "anything we heard from her husband should be as well written down for herself" (CAFN2-fn: 0446). And one husband was particularly defiant:

This man initially drove me out of his house, telling me that I have no right to interview his wife first without taking permission from him. I had to beg him and explain things in the most judicious way before he would allow me in. (CAFN2-fn: 1668)

The questioning then proceeded, but the man remained "skeptical" and contemptuous.

Another man "refused to let his wives answer for themselves; he answered for them" (CAFN1-br: p. 36). An old woman likewise insisted on answering for all the women in her house, "as they were wives of her children" (CAFN1-br: p. 23).

Some fieldworkers proved adept at confronting this kind of situation. From a CAFN3 interviewer:

Wife was later interviewed. She wanted not to answer at first, since husband has been interviewed. But on telling her that she might have her own opinion, they co-operated well and also gave me an interesting time.   (CAFN3-fn: 0089)

And in Owo, CAFN2 fieldworkers "moved together," partly because respondents "tended to crowd together, and since these are confidential interviews we had to trap each person in a different corner on getting to the house" (CAFN2-dr: p. 9).

"She said such questions her mother even cannot ask her"

Finally, Yoruba culture is imbued with the "strong conviction that individual behavior is not generally a matter for probing and comment" (Caldwell and Caldwell, 1978: 12).[4] Despite assurances that the interrogation "was nothing dangerous" (CAFN2-fn: 0547), many respondents found questions too personal to be tolerated—"immoral to their hearing" (CAFN1-br: p. 9). As a CAFN1 supervisor reported:

One woman refused bluntly to answer the questions. . . . We begged and petted her to answer, but she would not, saying that she cannot just answer some of the questions, that they were too personal. We thanked her and left.   (CAFNI-br: p. 6)

Other examples:

In one particular house a woman was annoyed when I talked to her about contraception. She said the first lady did not ask her such questions that her mother even cannot ask her. I tried to cool her down, but all efforts proved abortive.   (CAFNI-br: p. 5)

This respondent proved too difficult as far as questions relating to her children [are] concerned and would not give any detail about her husband except under general discussion. I found her very uncompromising.   (CAFN2-fn: 1731)

Reluctance to discuss contraception or even ideal family size is a persistent theme in the data, with respondents having to be "begged and cajoled before they would answer" (CAFN1-br: p. 23). Problems created by question sensitivity were particularly apparent in CAFN1, "The Beginning of Family Limitation," whose purpose was to measure the incidence of deliberate fertility control attempts and the circumstances under which these emerged. To that effect, researchers sampled Ibadan Yoruba women between the ages of 15 and 59, using a two-part interview schedule. The final question of Part A asked whether the subject had ever deliberately controlled her fertility: "Have you ever tried either to prevent a birth or to postpone it by any means?" (CAFN1-Q. 13). In the interview schedule the question was followed by a note to the fieldworker saying that this was the central question of the survey because the answer would determine whether the questioning would continue to Part B.[5]

But getting positive responses proved difficult. Of the 6,606 women interviewed, only 1,050 or one-sixth said they had used some method of family planning other than sexual abstinence and were therefore willing to complete Part B. Typically, supervisors accompanied interviewers on second visits to difficult subjects. Often they reported that "despite the fact that I joked with them and played with their children in order to get the second part, they said that they have told [the first interviewer] the truth" (CAFN1-br: p. 3). One interviewer summarized a common situation: "So if I finished part 'A' and turned to part 'B' they would refuse totally to answer that part" (CAFN1-br: p. 21).

Overall, maintaining subject compliance proved troublesome enough that fieldworkers were inclined to remark on situations where respondents "answered all the questions without any grudge" (CAFN2-fn: 1373). "Good" subjects provided "the information without much begging" (CAFN2-fn: 1225) and gave "full information concerning the situation" (CAFN2-fn: 1291). The "good" respondent was willing to "declare all the facts required from her without any question" (CAFN2-fn: 0450). Nevertheless, if subjects "hesitated at first," their reluctance was characteristically met with "more explanations" that resulted in eventual compliance (CAFN2-fn: 1220).

Invading Subjects' Territorial Selves

Gaining entrance required invading subjects' privacy, or "territorial selves" (cf. Goffman, 1971: 51–82). By observing subjects within their homes, interviewers accessed personal information that was neither directly nor freely offered. The project's principal researchers consciously utilized this advantage. For example, CAFN1 fieldworkers were directed as follows:

> While you are interviewing you should try to make sure that the information the woman is giving you is consistent (i.e. it does not contradict). For example, if she tells you that she always abstains for three (3) years after having a child and then you notice she has a child of one year old and that she is not abstaining at the moment, question her more closely to try and get the truth. ("Notice to All Interviewers," App. B, #15)

CAFN3 interviewers were instructed first to ask subjects whether they had any reason to doubt their fertility (CAFN3-Q.28a) and next to give their own opinion from observation and informal conversation with the respondent (Q.28b).

The scientists' ability to encroach upon subjects' selves evidenced their relatively greater force. Effectively patrolling one's territory requires power: "In general, the higher the rank, the greater the size of all territories of the self" (Goffman, 1971: 65). Moreover, the interviewer claimed authority to direct the interaction. The encounter would not be a reciprocal, "everyday" conversation in which information could be exchanged. Some subjects did attempt dialogue with an interviewer:

> This man was very helpful, especially when I read the questionnaire as if it was Americans who want a comparative study of this society and theirs. He answered the questions enthusiastically, and at the end, wanted to know what is the considered opinion of Americans on this question: "Wealth and children— do you think that those things are obtained through one's efforts or by the grace of Allah?" (CAFN2-fn: 1174)

As a rule, however, respondents were expected only to answer the questions put. In this way, interviewees were subjected to one-way scrutiny, observations from which researchers were officially exempt.

Subjects who expected an everyday conversation were disappointed in another way as well. Goffman (1959: 9–10, 13–14, 58) has pointed out that in ordinary interaction actors tacitly agree to accept each other's definitions and claims; tactfully they exchange "performed cues on faith." This was not the case with regard to CAFN; fieldworkers felt free—in fact, duty bound—to challenge subjects. For instance, CAFN1 subjects who said they had never tried to control their fertility were often revisited by the fieldworker, sometimes in the company of her supervisor, in order to get at the "truth." CAFN interviews, then (like all professional interviews), evidenced discrepant levels of disclosure and power.

If human action is staged by performers, we can refer to the space (Goffman, 1959: 107) and time (Giddens, 1984: 122) in which a performance is given as the "front region." A "back region" is that sequestered space and time in which a performer can relax and "step out of character"; moreover, the back region is where "illusions and impressions are openly constructed" (Goffman, 1959: 112). According to Giddens (1984: 122–24), control over regionalization shapes the situation and degree of one's presence-availability. Put another way, autonomous actors manipulate front and back regions in order to patrol their information preserves.

Because questioning took place within their everyday-life space and time, CAFN subjects had little recourse to back regions in which to muster energy or plan front-region decorum. Typically, interviews occurred in respondents' homes and without advance appointments. For example, in one reported instance the subject was sleeping when approached but "got up to answer the questions" (CAFN1-fn: 1194). Fieldworkers, by contrast, had the advantage of late-night "steering group" discussions (described in Chapter 3)—back-region occasions for what Goffman (1959: 175–76) has referred to as "staging talk": "In the early days interest centered on how to investigate the research topic in a more revealing way and how to adapt approaches and amend questions; later the focus shifted to improving the quality of field and processing work" (Okediji et al., 1976: 135). During staging talk (never in the presence of an audience), "the reception given one's performance is mulled over; . . . wounds are licked and morale is strengthened for the next performance" (Goffman, 1959: 176).

The postcolonial right-to-invade rested on the relatively greater strength of scientists' bureaucratically orchestrated performance team. As Erving Goffman (1959: 92) has pointed out, performance teams can confront one another and struggle to impose contending definitions upon a situation. CAFN subjects had their own definitions of the entrance-gaining endeavor. Some found it simply curious:

> Many respondents wondered why such [an] elaborate study had to be done on their family patterns. Many have put it down as one of the curiosities of "Oyinbos" or White men, while many more said it is a result of having not enough to do. (CAFNI-br: p. 38)

Largely, however, respondents saw the experience as an unwelcome intrusion into their everyday activities: too long, abrasive in its bureaucratic affiliation and organization, and contrary to privacy values.

But subjects, unlike the fieldworkers, had little back-region space or time in which to enclose themselves or to form competitive teams, let alone prepare a practiced performance. Only the principal researchers could purposefully mold, train, and direct a team of subordinates who had at their disposal the cultural capital of both Western and indigenous society.

Conclusion

Schutz (1970: 239) has pointed to the expanding "anonymity of partners" as a seminal characteristic of modernity: "Our own social surrounding is within the reach of everyone, everywhere; an anonymous other, whose goals are unknown to us because of his anonymity, may bring us, together with our system of interests and relevances, within his control. We are less and less masters in our own right to define what is, and what is not, relevant to us." CAFN subjects must have felt this way as leagues of unfamiliar fieldworkers converged upon their neighborhoods and villages, invading both their "conversational preserves" (that is, violating expectations that they themselves might control who could summon them into talk and when) and their "information preserves" (specifying questions to be answered).

As a consequence, the exercise proved problematic. Subjects were "difficult to maneuver." Some ran away or refused to allow field-workers into their homes; others made excuses. A few were "rough," aggressively turning interviewers out, requesting that they not return and promising "insult" if they did.

Armed with both Western and Yoruba cultural capital, however, fieldworkers tended to be successful in gaining entrance and com-pleting interviews. Relatively greater team power allowed CAFN researchers to define the extraction of information from resistant in-digenous subjects as legitimate. This was a first step in establishing bureaucratic surveillance of these Yoruba respondents.

Compliance in bureaucratic surveillance can mean making oneself available to other "representations of public morality" or "lessons" (Foucault, 1975: 110) as well. The CAFN projects carried fertility-related lessons that challenged Yoruba views and introduced the Western "taken-for-granted." The next chapter explores these les-sons.

5 The Lessons
Inherent in the
CAFN Projects

To gain entrance in Ilawe-Ekiti, fieldworkers introduced themselves in the churches and explained that "our Project is educative" (CAFN2-dr: p. 10). It was. The interview schedules schooled interviewees and interviewers alike in First World "representations of public morality," or "lessons" (Foucault, 1975: 110–11). For most respondents the lessons were relatively unfamiliar; for the fieldworkers they reinforced prior learning in Western attitudes and behavior.

Disciplining Power and Docile Bodies

Michel Foucault has traced the means of social control from the public spectacles of torture used throughout the Middle Ages to the "disciplinary power" developed during the seventeenth and eighteenth centuries. Disciplinary power derives from hierarchical observation—bureaucratic surveillance—coupled with widely circulated representations of acceptable public morality. Moreover, disciplinary power is expansive, undertaking to control more and more areas of human behavior until ultimately "the whole indefinite domain of the non-conforming is punishable" (Foucault, 1975: 178–79). In short, disciplinary power employs bureaucratically monitored lessons in the normative to produce not just law-abiding citizens but "docile bodies" (Foucault, 1975: 138). Prototypical locales for disciplinary power were the military, the industrialized workplace, and the school. In the twentieth century, world-system science (see Chapter 1) became an agent of disciplinary power.

To be effective, representations of acceptable public morality must be circulated as widely and repeated as often as possible; they must find their way into everyday conversation (Foucault, 1975: 108–11). The CAFN interviews were occasions for such circulation and repetition: that is, they became lesson-bearing instruments.

Generally, these lessons challenged (however inadvertently) the taken-for-granted of everyday Yoruba life. For example, in a society in which high fertility is seen as a divine reward and evidence of right living (Caldwell and Caldwell, 1987: 415), respondents were asked, "Would you regard it as a tragedy if you were not succeeded by descendants?" (CAFN3-Q.20i). And in a world that views barrenness as fundamentally abhorrent (Caldwell and Caldwell, 1987), subjects were asked to enumerate "the good things about having no children at all" (CAFN2-Q.47a).[1] Moreover, the interviews directly introduced the Western value of relativism. For instance, respondents were assured at the onset that "there is no right or wrong answer." But the relativism inherent in this "value-free" position is, of course, itself a value in opposition to the religio-cultural fundamentalism of traditional Yoruba beliefs. Meanwhile (and ironically), a Western definition was often put to subjects not as one of several equally valid ways of viewing a situation but as *the* legitimate or "real" way of doing so. For example, it was assumed that "education" referred to formal Western schooling, not to socialization in traditional skills such as hunting, farming, or drumming.

In introducing the Western taken-for-granted, the interviews carried lessons antithetical to the traditional religio-cultural absolutism that supports high fertility among the Yoruba. This chapter describes the following five representations of Western morality, or lessons, inherent in the CAFN projects:

1. The "real" family is the nuclear family.
2. Children should be consciously evaluated according to a cost calculus.

3. Western contraceptive methods are as morally acceptable as traditional measures.
4. Personal efficacy is normal and natural.
5. Placing oneself under bureaucratic surveillance is normal and natural.

Taken together, these lessons constitued social structural, contraceptive, and attitudinal messages that legitimated the social construction of purposefully limited family size.

Lesson 1: The "Real" Family Is the Nuclear Family

Caldwell holds that a primary prerequisite to Third World fertility decline is family nucleation, the process by which the traditional joint family gives way to the relationship-oriented conjugal unit valued in First World societies (see Chapter 7). Insofar as family nucleation has occurred in Nigeria, considerable responsibility for it may be assigned to the Western school system: "In primary school, children are taught about a family unit consisting of a father, mother and children, the parents being primarily devoted to rearing the children" (Caldwell, 1977a: 15).

CAFN interviews taught a similar lesson. For instance, the women who were willing to answer Part B of CAFN1 (that is, those who said they had used means other than abstinence to limit or space their children) heard that it can be all right not to be influenced by the extended family. Consider the following question sequence:

Which relatives or other persons know that you have been practising contraception?
Which relatives or other persons have encouraged you to practise contraception?
Which relatives or other persons have been against you[r] practising contraception?
What did they say?
Were you ever influenced by them to stop practising contraception? (CAFN1-Q.26a–e)

The lesson was that although some relatives may not approve of a woman's practicing contraception, their opinions need not necessarily influence her.

Further, in a culture in which "the centrality of the lineage leaves the conjugal family unusually weak" and the sexes typically segregated, even residentially (Caldwell and Caldwell, 1987: 419), respondents were questioned about their marital "relationship," a Western concept. In a semistructured, precoded question (see Appendix A), subjects were asked, "How would you describe the relationship between yourself and your husband/wife?" (CAFN2-Q.26).[2] They were further questioned as to whether they "usually live" together or "sleep in the same room or house or compound," as well as whether they ate together, sat together at parties or other celebrations, or visited friends together.[3]

Then too, the foster care of children is institutionalized in Yoruba kinship structure and tradition. To facilitate their weaning, permit their school attendance, or enable them to help with chores, children may live intermittently with relatives other than their biological parents. Children belong to the lineage as much as to a particular mother, who is one of several entrusted with their care (Riesman, 1986: 105). Accordingly, the sending out and taking in of children is routine among rural and urban, wealthy and poor parents (Caldwell 1976a: 219–20; Caldwell and Caldwell, 1987: 419; Isiugo-Abanihe, 1985: 56). Within this context, CAFN2 (Q. 14–15) and CAFN3 (Q. 5a–b) asked, "How many of *your own children* are now living with you?" and "How many of *your own children* are now living elsewhere?" Subsequent questions (CAFN2-Q.19 and 20a) required subjects to explain why any children not their "own" might be staying with them and why any of their "own" children might be living elsewhere. The questions were designed to measure the incidence of and reasons for fosterage in Yorubaland. But this concept is itself Western imposition: Only when the "real" family is nuclear are children "fostered."[4]

Lesson 2: Children Should Be Evaluated According to a Cost Calculus

The research required subjects to explicate the rewards and costs of having children. For example, respondents were asked "what would be the good things" and "what would be the bad things" about becoming pregnant in the next two years (CAFN1-Q.29b–c) or about "having a/another baby this year" (CAFN2-Q.42–43).

Moreover, although material things have relatively little importance in traditional African culture—they do not replace human relationships (Riesman, 1986: 105) and cannot be balanced against the value of children. Nevertheless, the research required subjects to think first in terms of the direct rewards and costs of children:

> We are interested in how much money children earn and how much they contribute to the family in other ways by helping with farming or trading or other things. We know that children also must cost something and that the family must spend money on them. We are going to ask you some questions on these matters.   (CAFN2-Q.50a)

Having answered those questions, respondents were next required to weigh costs against rewards:

> We have just asked you several questions about the value of the work children do and also about how much the children cost the family. We would like you to think about these matters and to see if you can compare the value of children's earnings and the work they do with the amount of money the family has to spend on them.
>
> *Question:* Do you think that the money spent on children (all children under 18 years of age) is more than the value of their earnings and productive work or is less? That is, do you think children make parents financially better off or worse off? (CAFN2-Q.50b)[5]

This question was followed by one requiring further calculation and greater detail:

The last question was probably hard to answer because we included together all kinds of children—old ones and young ones, girls and boys, children who go to school and children who do not. In the next questions we try to separate them into different groups. In each case we want to know if children of this kind have to have more money spent on them than the value of their work and earnings (parents worse off) or if their work and earnings [are] worth more than the money spent on them (parents better off). (CAFN2-Q.50c)

Beyond these direct cost calculations, respondents were asked to think about what their children prevented them from having or doing; that is, they were taught to weigh and balance "opportunity costs":

If you did have a/another child this year, would you be richer or poorer in the future?
(If "poorer") What do you think you would have to do without if you had another child this year?
If you had another baby this year, would it inconvenience you? Would it stop you doing things which you would otherwise have done? What things? (CAFN2-Q.44a–c)

Further, the questionnaires taught parents to weigh the value of children against alternative (chiefly material) "goods":

What would you like to be able to have in the following list if you could only afford one? If you could afford a second, what would it be? What about a third?
1. a new car
2. a second-hand lorry
3. a new house
4. another child
5. a lot of new furniture
6. a university education for one of your children
7. a trip to England
8. more education for yourself
9. a lot of new clothes   (CAFN2-Q.37)

Subsequently, the alternative suggested was money:

> If the Government (or someone else) said that they would pay
> you money not to have any more children once you had four
> living children, how much money would it take before you
> would agree?   (CAFN2-Q.40)

Lesson 3: Western Contraceptive Methods Are as Morally Acceptable as Traditional Measures

The interviews made no moral distinction between Western birth
control methods and abstinence or other traditional contraceptive
measures. For example:

> Have you ever used any method of family planning or contra-
> ception? Have you ever tried to stop yourself from conceiving?
> Have you stopped sexual relations after the birth of a child?
> Have you used contraceptives (pills, condoms, diaphragms,
> I.U.D.s, foams, jellies, etc.) or rhythm or withdrawal? (If YES)
> Are you still using them?   (CAFN2-Q.28)[6]

This question placed abstinence within the same moral category as
contraceptives that were often considered immoral among the Yoruba
(Caldwell and Caldwell, 1987: 414). Furthermore, the questionnaires
not only presented Western contraceptives as taken-for-granted but
also educated both subjects and interviewers about them.[7] CAFN1
(Q.13) required interviewers to explain and discuss "the whole list of
[contraceptive] possibilities, each one individually." The question:

> Have you ever tried either to prevent a birth or to postpone it by
> any means? Have you ever used any of the following:
> FOR EACH METHOD.   Code 1. Yes used.   2. Never used but
> heard of it.   3. Never heard of it.   4. Refused [to answer].
>> (i) postponing pregnancy after a birth by having no sexual
>> relations
>> (ii) having no sexual relations for more than 2 years after
>> a birth
>> (iii) using charms sold by a native doctor

(iv) using medicines sold by a native doctor

(v) using rhythm (i.e. sexual relations at only certain times between periods)

(vi) using withdrawal (coitus interruptus)

(vii) using condoms

(viii) using jellies, creams, quinine pessaries

(ix) using douching, washing with salt water

(x) using diaphragm, Dutch cap

(xi) using foams, foaming tablets

(xii) using Grafenberg or other internal rings

(xiii) using pills (oral contraceptives)

(xiv) I.U.D. (loop, coil)

(xv) husband sterilized by doctor (i.e. vasectomy)

(xvi) wife sterilized by doctor to prevent pregnancies

(xvii) abortion performed by doctor

(xviii) abortion performed by yourself

(xix) abortion performed by someone not a doctor

(xx) Other (write in) _____

With the addition of "having injections every month or every few months," CAFN3 (Q.6) presented a similar list.

Although the number of subjects who refused to respond was negligible (less than 1 percent), the proportions of those saying they had "never heard of it" was substantial (Table 5.1 presents the percentages of CAFN1 respondents for each method listed). There is some irony in the possible response category 3, "Never heard of it," since "the whole list of possibilities" had been thoroughly explained and discussed, "each one individually," before the answers were recorded. Even respondents who had previously heard of each method were drilled in the information.[8]

Lesson 4: Personal Efficacy Is Normal and Natural

Traditional West African cultures stress acceptance of or harmony with divinity and nature above personal agency, or instrumentality (Asante, 1987; Riesman, 1986). Questions such as the following challenged this view:

Table 5.1. CAFN1 Respondents Who "Never Heard of" Various
Contraceptive Methods

Contraceptive Method	Percentage (N = 6,606)
Temporary abstinence after a birth	0.2
Abstinence for more than two years after a birth	0.8
Charms sold by native doctor	25.0
Medicines sold by native doctor	26.1
Rhythm (sexual relations at infertile times between periods)	30.0
Withdrawal (*coitus interruptus*)	45.6
Condoms	45.0
Jellies, creams, quinine pessaries	74.8
Douches, washing with salt water	63.6
Diaphragm, Dutch cap	59.4
Foams, foaming tablets	70.4
Grafenberg or other internal rings	70.8
Pills (oral contraceptives)	16.8
IUD (loop, coil)	42.2
Husband's sterilization by doctor (vasectomy)	77.1
Wife's sterilization by doctor	56.5
Abortion performed by doctor	7.1
Abortion performed by yourself	8.0
Abortion performed by someone else (not a doctor)	9.7

Do you think a woman should have a lot of children? Is it possible to have too many? What would you say would be too many? (CAFN2-Q.30)

A husband and wife have five sons and no daughter and wonder whether this is enough children. What would you do in this situation?

A husband and wife have five daughters and no son and wonder whether this is enough children. What would you do in this situation? (CAFN2-Q.31b, i–ii)

Would you rather have ten children or six children altogether? (CAFN2-Q.45a)[9]

The reinforcement of personal efficacy as normal and natural was particularly apparent throughout CAFN1, Part B. For example:

When you made up your mind to use family planning, what were the circumstances that made you come to this decision? Why did you do it? What happened at that time? (CAFN1-Q.16)

These respondents further heard that they could make individual decisions, without their husband's knowledge or consent:

Did your husband/man know you were using a method when you first started?

When you first thought about using family planning, did you talk about it to your husband/man? (CAFN1-Q.22c, 23)[10]

In a few instances the efficacy lesson was combined with that of the nuclear family to yield lessons in parental responsibility, Western style:

Some people would rather have four children than eight. Why do you think they feel this way?

Is it as easy to educate eight children as four?

Why? (CAFN2-Q.46a–b)

The following question not only presumed efficacy (along with conjugal decision-making) but also taught acceptable reasons for an antinatal choice:

If you and your husband/wife decided it would be better not to have another child for some reason (because of money, or because of housing difficulties, or because you wanted to move elsewhere, or because it might affect your health or the baby's), would you be very disappointed? (CAFN2-Q.23)[11]

According to Foucault (1975: 104–6), disciplinary power requires a "technology of representation" whereby aberrations from the normative are represented to the masses as disadvantageous because subsequent negative consequences will outweigh rewards. CAFN questions explicate Foucault's point. Problems were presented as logically necessary consequences of having too many children. Consider, for example, the following hypothetical situation, presented to CAFN2 subjects:

> A man is living in a big town with two wives and twelve children. Because he can afford only two rooms, his wives and children are complaining because they think there is not enough space. He would like all his children to go to school but can afford to let only a few do so. How do you think they got into this situation?   (CAFN2-Q.31a)

A follow-up question asked, "What should they do about it?"[12]

Such questions were lessons in the value of small families. An alternative scenario provided by one subject offers an instructive comparison:

> The respondent . . . is one of the lucky women in the world. She told me that she has 10 children, one died. Among the remaining 9 children she has two doctors of medicine, one doctor of Book (Ph.D. Geography), two engineers, one nurse and two teachers. So she believes that one should have many children. (CAFN2-fn: 1238)

The scientists' scenario instructed subjects in the negative consequences (lack of sufficient space and unfulfilled ambitions for one's children) of having too many children and implied that the actors got into this situation by decisions they made or failed to make. In contrast, the respondent's scenario implied the positive value of a large family and revealed an absence of a sense of personal efficacy. In sum, the scenario presented by the scientists asked respondents to view parenting in terms of costs, while that presented by the subject pointed to eventual rewards.

Lesson 5: Placing Oneself under Bureaucratic Surveillance Is Normal and Natural

As data introduced in Chapter 4 indicate, CAFN took for granted and taught separation of the individual from family authority and concomitant cooperation in bureaucratic surveillance. The process of gaining entrance evidenced instruction in appropriate secondary role behavior. This lesson persisted throughout the interviews as fieldworkers and respondents continued to interact primarily according to the "rules" of secondary roles.

Furthermore, the research schooled participants in the legitimacy of self-categorization: fieldworkers placed subjects—or asked subjects to place themselves—in scientifically contrived categories. Respondents were questioned about their highest level of (Western) education, for example—an imposed bureaucratic category.

Then too, the scientific paradigm necessitated "securing satisfactorily quantifiable answers, especially relating to ages and dates" (Caldwell and Ware, 1977: 489).[13] Consequently, subjects were required to define or locate themselves by age, another concept peculiar to the penetrating culture. International standard time is a social construction that accompanied the global spread of bureaucratic organization (Zerubavel, 1982). Age as measured on the Gregorian calendar is a cultural imposition in Yorubaland (Caldwell and Igun, 1971: 287; Caldwell and Ware, 1977: 489).[14] Because some familiarity with and acceptance of bureaucratically constructed secondary roles and categorization are necessary for the promotion of Western birth control methods in Yorubaland, this lesson was instrumental in the social reconstruction of "reasonable"—that is, purposefully limited—family size.

Afrocentrist scholar Molefi Kete Asante (1987: 184) has argued that the "bias of categorization," which shuffles people into bureaucratically prescribed roles and categories, is a Western notion. In contrast, the holistic world view found in traditional Africa promulgates spiritual commitment to harmony with others in primary relationships. But the CAFN research drilled participants in bureaucratic categorization.

Conclusion

With the imposition of bureaucratic surveillance came disciplinary power as Yorubas became subject to First World "representations of public morality" or "lessons" (Foucault, 1975: 110). This persistent process, which began with colonization, is evident in the CAFN interview schedules. The questionnaires implicitly challenged taken-for-granted assumptions of everyday Yoruba life—matters of kinship loyalty and religio-cultural fundamentalism—and introduced Western scientific relativism as a value.

The five lessons described in this chapter were representations of public morality in support of purposefully limited family size. Subjects heard that they could determine whether children were more costly than rewarding and could escape the traditional family surveillance system—with its fundamentalistic representations of public morality—in the Western idea of a value-free world. They might choose to do so if they were willing to use Western contraceptives, to take some control over their procreative lives, and to submit themselves to the playing of categorized bureaucratic roles. The following chapter explores subjects' resistance to these lessons.

6   Resisting the Lessons

Confronted with "nonfitting" values or beliefs, individuals attempt to deflect or resist them (Festinger, 1957). Because the lessons inherent in CAFN were First World cultural impositions, many subjects saw the interview experience as an attack on African values and resisted CAFN's lessons. As recounted in Chapter 4, some refused to be questioned at all. Even where interviewers successfully gained entrance, compliance was not necessarily ongoing: "She was nice at the beginning but later she refused to answer any of the questions" (CAFN3-fn: 0033); "She said that there are some of the questions which are probing too much into one's private life after she had agreed to talk" (CAFN2-fn: 2179).

Questions that subjects found fairly innocuous, such as whether they had ever married or what their usual job was, had low no-response rates. As fieldworkers encroached further on respondents' informational selves, however, the subjects recoiled, rebuffing the questions, and no-response rates climbed. This was particularly true among those who had not attended Western schools. Some "very difficult" subjects not only "would not answer my questions" but "tried to stop others doing so" (CAFN1-br: p. 20). According to one account, "We earlier enjoyed the co-operation of the Landlord in the house, but the women pressurised him to a breakdown towards the end" (CAFN2-dr: p. 11).

Respondents resisted not only by refusing to answer certain questions but also by reaffirming that fertility decisions were "up to God," by elucidating specific reasons for having large families, and, more generally, by restating the traditional Yoruba case. Just as CAFN interviewers marched into the field with both the legacy of and the cultural capital necessary to invasion, so also CAFN subjects armed themselves with the cultural capital necessary to resistance. This chapter examines subjects' ways of resisting the five CAFN lessons, then examines the relationship between Western schooling and respondent compliance.

"I strongly suspect that she lied"

Among the protective means likely to be used by the more dependent actors in any dialectic of control are lying and trickery. Anthropologists (e.g., Bleek, 1987; Nachman, 1984; Salamone, 1977) recognize that Third World subjects lie to researchers as a "strategy for survival, a code to preserve . . . self-respect" (Bleek, 1987: 319). In the words of a Tiv informant, "When I read what the white man has written of our customs, I laugh, for it is the custom of our people to lie as a matter of course to outsiders, especially the white man. We ask, 'Why does he want to know such personal things about us?'" (quoted in Bleek, 1987: 320–21; and Salamone, 1977: 117). Lying to invaders is a form of Yoruba resistance that dates back to British colonialization. As C. L. Temple described the situation, "The natives very naturally thought that if they launched a sufficient number of lies they could prevent their conquerors from getting to know anything about them and, perchance, so confuse their minds that they would give up the attempt in disgust and go away" (1918: 104).

With similar motives, some CAFN subjects apparently lied to protect their informational selves, as suspicious interviewers reported: "I strongly suspect that she lied about her marital status and education" (CAFN2-fn: 0540); "I just feel she refuses to tell some truth" (CAFN2-fn: 0583); "I am convinced that he did not give the accurate number of his children and wives" (CAFN2-fn: 0425); "I suspected she had used one type of contraceptive, but she would not tell" (CAFN1-br: p. 5); "I later discovered that the respondent was not truthful" (CAFN2-fn: 2169).[1] In one fieldworker's summary, "They don't always tell the truth" (CAFN1-br: p. 20).

Closely related to lying is telling interviewers what the respondents presume they want to hear. The documents do not offer direct evidence of this practice. But given traditional Yoruba attitudes, some of the answers to the question about how the man with two wives, twelve children, too little space, and not enough money got into such a situation (Chapter 5) make one wonder:

He has no foresight and should have thought of this problem before he started having so many children. (CAFN2-sr: 2160)

The man must be a womaniser and a polygynist who cannot control his desire for sex. (CAFN2-sr: 2180)

It must be a covetous polygamous idiot, who cannot limit himself to his resources. (CAFN2-sr: 2169)

Greediness is the acquisition of children. (CAFN2-sr: 2281)

Trickery and evasion were further forms of Yoruba cultural capital that could be used against outsiders. The name Yoruba itself means "cunning" (Bascom, 1969: 5), and according to legend the Yoruba were so named by their northern neighbors, the Hausa (Fadipe, 1970: 30). "Quite a variety of tricks and shifts [were] brought into play" in Yoruba culture: for instance, in the marketplace vendors employed dented measuring containers, while a buyer might insist on measuring a purchase him- or herself and use a hand to support flour that towered over the top (Fadipe, 1970: 163). Temple (1918: 128) complained of the Yoruba's "stinting the white man when he wanted to make himself disagreeable." And Isichei (1983: 42) has described how Nigerians foiled British attempts to introduce cotton plantations by boiling the seeds before planting them.

CAFN interviewers too were met with various "tricks and shifts." "Some made appointments and didn't keep them" (CAFN1-br: pp. 24, 30), or, as one fieldworker complained:

> They told me to return in the evening, but when I did they still said they were not ready to answer my questions. I went there three times. (CAFN1-br: p. 30)

Beside failing to keep appointments, subjects protected themselves by "making jest" or finding the questions "funny" or "ridiculous" (CAFN2-fn: 1163, 1176, 1177; CAFN2-dr: p. 34). Others used distraction and "irrelevance": "She at times sets another question for herself, i.e., she answered not the question put to her but engaged in irrelevance" (CAFN2-fn: 1732); "He is fond of using [a] question in answering other questions" (CAFN1-fn: 1395). And at least one interviewer met with a combination of these tactics:

> Some would give me an appointment to come in the evening if it happened I was there in the morning. On getting there in the evening they would ask me irrelevant questions which did not even pertain to my missions there. (CAFN1-br: p. 7)

"This attitude is foreign to African society"

Some respondents seemed willing to confront fieldworkers more directly, however. To questions implying that the "real" family is nuclear, at least one subject pointed (apparently with irritation) to the foreign nature of the concept "conjugal relationship":

> He said that he has not eaten with his wives and that he will never do that. He continued in saying that this attitude is foreign to African society. This is a thing well known among the Europeans, he added. (CAFN2-fn: 1358)

More often, subjects pointed to the viability of the lineage, or extended family. For instance, asked what the man who had too many children should do about his plight, subjects over and over again said that one option was to "seek the help of some relatives" (CAFN2-sr: pp. 6–7). For the most part, this kind of help meant sending some or all of the children "to their grandparents or to brothers and sisters around" or "distributing" them "among relatives who have less responsibility" or are "more privileged" (CAFN2-sr: pp. 6–7). (Interestingly, respondents never used the term "foster care" in their explanations; as Chapter 5 points out, "fostering" is a Western concept.)

Respondents also pointed to the "sibling education chain": "She has educated the older 2 children and wants them to send the younger 2 to school" (CAFN3-fn: 0190). Similarly:

He cannot find a reason for educating all the children one has but to educate a few and [let] the others [be] educated by their brothers and sisters.   (CAFN2-fn: 2156)

In presenting the traditional Yoruba case with regard to fosterage and the sibling educational chain, and in objecting to the concept "conjugal relationship" as culturally imposed, subjects reaffirmed the traditional view that the "real" family was the lineage.

"The poor man must not lack both wealth and children"

Many respondents balked at explicating the rewards and costs of having children. Asked to elucidate the "good things" about becoming pregnant in the next two years, one-third of CAFN1 respondents replied only that they wanted another baby. Half either said "nothing" or "don't know," or refused to respond.[2] Similarly, when asked to discuss the "bad things" about becoming pregnant in the next two years, two-thirds of CAFN1 subjects would say only "nothing" or "don't know," or that it had not been long enough since the last birth. The proportions of CAFN2 respondents' replies to similar questions were much the same. The vast majority of respondents, then, resisted practicing the cost calculus urged by those two questions. As one fieldworker pointed out in describing a subject's response to the CAFN2 question whether his children had produced more wealth than they had cost:

His thought is children are wealth. His opinion is that a poor man should have many children since he is not rich; that is, the poor man must not lack both wealth and children. (CAFN2-fn: 1907)

Table 6.1 gives the percentages of men and women who refused to answer selected CAFN2 questions. As the reader can see from

Table 6.1. CAFN2 Respondents Refusing to Answer Selected Questions

Question	Males ($N = 1,497$)	Females ($N = 1,499$)	Total ($N = 2,996$)
Ever married?	0.1%	0.0%	<0.1%
Usual job?	0.3	0.2	0.2
Number of live births?	0.5	0.7	0.6
Number of wives in household?	1.4	1.1	1.2
Prefer 6 or 10 children in all?	1.3	2.5	2.0
What religion?	2.8	3.4	3.1
Advantages of 10 children over 6?	6.0	8.7	7.3
Main reasons people are infertile?	7.8	9.1	8.4
Prefer 10 or 6 children?	8.3	11.7	10.1
Good things about a birth this year?	12.3	11.5	11.9
Bad things about a birth this year?	13.4	13.2	13.3
A birth this year an inconvenience?	13.0	13.8	13.4
Richer or poorer if you had another child this year?	19.9	22.0	21.0

Note: These percentages do not include "Don't Know" or "Nothing" responses.

that table, just over one-fifth refused to speculate about whether they would be richer or poorer in the future if they had another child that year. Asked whether another child might inconvenience them and how, 13.4 percent refused to respond. These are high no-response rates when compared with those of more innocuous questions, such as whether the respondent was ever married.

Table 6.2, giving subjects' responses, by gender, as to whether another baby this year might be an inconvenience, shows that those who were willing to specify the inconvenience were in the minority (32.7 percent). Another 3.4 percent said it probably would be but could not specify in what way. Over 46 percent of the sample (50.4 percent of men and 42.1 percent of women) said that another child would be no inconvenience; and 13.4 percent refused to answer altogether.

When CAFN2 subjects were asked what they would choose if they could afford only one item from a list that included a new car, a new house, another child, and a trip to England (see Chapter 5), 29 per-

Table 6.2. Inconvenience of Another Baby This Year

	Males (N = 1,497)	Females (N = 1,499)	Total (N = 2,996)
Inconvenience in			
social life	8.3%	7.7%	8.0%
traveling	1.2	0.9	1.1
finances	2.0	0.9	1.4
studies	4.6	5.4	5.0
work	7.3	16.5	11.8
other	4.6	6.1	5.4
Subtotal	28.0	37.5	32.7
No inconvenience	50.4	42.1	46.3
Probably, but don't know how	3.3	3.5	3.4
Not married, therefore problems	5.3	3.1	4.2
No response	13.0	13.8	13.4
Subtotal	72.0	62.5	67.3
Total	100%	100%	100%

Note: Percentages calculated from responses to CAFN2 Question 44c: If you had another baby this year, would it inconvenience you? Would it stop you doing things which you would otherwise have done? What things?

cent pointed out that one doesn't have to "afford" a child. Asked how much money it would take before they would agree not to have more than four living children, 72 percent either named an outrageous sum or said they would not accept money. Twenty-eight percent said they would not accept money. Forty-four percent said more than 20,000 *naira*, an amount 500 times the sample's average monthly income, or over forty years' average earnings—and even this response did not tell the whole story. In the words of one fieldworker:

She finds it difficult to answer Q.40 but . . . finally decide[s] on the maximum of half a million *naira* and a minimum of 100,000 *naira*. I just have to record [for her] the maximum of N20,000. (CAFN2-fn: 0647)

Beside balking at performing the calculative exercises, respondents raised considerations of their own regarding children's cost calculus. Some reminded interviewers of other-than-economic or practical rewards from children, such as community prestige:

> This man . . . fully understands that it is more economical to have a small size family but he only has interest in great number of children. His idea is that the great[er] the number of children one has, the [more] important the person is in the community. (CAFN1-fn: 0004)

Some pointed out that farm life allowed for and required many children:

> She insists on having many children so that one may have a large farm and plenty of children to work on the farm. . . . No problem of what to eat. One can therefore count the cost of living here to be a minimum.   (CAFN2-fn: 2044)

> He saw it was not too much for him to have ten children since not all will go to school or read too far. As long as his farm products yield well he has no barrier in maintaining the ten. Therefore family planning is meaningless to him.   (CAFN2-fn: 0668)

Others emphasized the eventual rewards of grown children, particularly for the old and poor:

> The man is fairly old. . . . He added that there is no good thing in having no children. He said that one should have descendant[s] and somebody to look after one at old age.   (CAFN2-fn: 2251)

> There is [the] possibility [that] one of the children will become rich, live long and see to the well-being of the parents when they are old.   (CAFN2-fn: 1907)

Many subjects argued, furthermore, that because of high infant and child mortality the potential value of any particular child was at risk:

> He said he would have loved to have only 4 children but have to make it 6 because he doesn't know how many of them would live.   (CAFN1-fn: 0069)

She said that she has seen a woman with four children only, and the four died within two years, and the woman is left without a child now. That is why she feels that one may have many. (CAFN2-fn: 2277)

This man . . . stressed the importance of having many children by his own example, wherein he had 22 births altogether and 11 of them died. Statistically speaking, he said there is every probability that all his children would have died if he had [had] only five. He therefore concluded that he cannot support the idea of family planning.   (CAFN2-fn: 1672)

One old woman took considerable time (as did her fieldworker) to elaborate this position:

This woman told me that "ABIKU" (children born to die) is a great problem in Nigeria, that the spirits keep on worrying us here so we can't escape it when giving birth to children. . . . A woman can give birth to 5 or 6 children and have some that will die. Imagine a case of a woman who is to give birth to nine children and only three will survive. I witnessed the occasion, [she said]; this was done through some certain power. So think of this. It is difficult to stop childbearing at a certain time because we don't know which [child] will be ours [to keep]. O.K. there is another case again [in] which the three stars of the family died and the parents were not having many children. What will the parents do? Only the small children [remain], and they can't give birth anymore. You know it's terrible to have 3 children graduate and [then] die within some months when they were already grown up. No one ever thought of this.   (CAFN3-fn: 0112)

There were other risks to be considered as well, such as the uncertainty of a child's educational or financial success:

One has to bear as many children as possible because . . . some may turn out to be failures in life, while some may succeed in life.   (CAFN2-sr: 2062)

The man was very frank. . . . he doesn't know how many of them would . . . turn out to be children whom parents could be proud of. (CAFN1-fn: 0069)

If one has lots of children some may be good and others may be bad, so that it's good to have as many as possible so that one can see responsible ones among them. (CAFN2-sr: 2166)

Finally, the following illustrates not only the traditional Yoruba position regarding risk but also the educative nature of the survey:

[The respondent believes that] it may be risky to have just [a] few children, since all of them may be snatched by the cold hand of death. I made her to realise that if one takes care of the few children and give[s] them medical attention, it is sure as death that they will not die. (CAFN2-fn: 2711)

Subjects deflected the idea, then, that children ought to be evaluated according to a cost calculus by refusing to comply in the calculative exercises and by pointing out considerations other than money in balancing the rewards of having children against the costs.

"She is not interested in such topics"

In responding to questions about birth control methods, many subjects took the occasion to point out that Western contraceptives, like conjugal relationships, were foreign cultural imports: "They said that they do not want birth control as it is against their tradition" (CAFN1-br: p. 8).[3] Some said that Western contraceptives were "looked on with scorn and contempt in their community" (CAFN2-fn: 1697) or that using them was immoral: "She told me it is a sin to use contraceptives and that one should accept the number of children one is given by God" (CAFN2-fn: 1689).

A large number of respondents were emphatic in their refusal to consider the use of modern contraceptives:

She was not finding questions about contraception . . . necessary to be asked, since she is not interested in such topics. (CAFN2-fn: 2189)

The respondent very much frown[ed] at the mention of birth control methods and said he would never practise it in life. (CAFN2-fn: 1423)

She . . . objected to the use of contraceptives. She told me she has never used one before and will never use one. (CAFN2-fn: 1689)

"Things should be allowed to happen as it pleases God"

Significant numbers refused to answer questions proceeding from the assumption that personal efficacy is normal and natural. Chapter 5 argued that expecting subjects to give specific numbers for ideal family size presumed personal efficacy. In response to number-eliciting questions, a relatively high proportion of subjects simply did not comply. Asked, for instance, whether they would prefer ten children or six (see Table 6.1), 10.1 percent of the CAFN2 sample either said they didn't know or refused to answer altogether. Again, this is a high no-response rate when compared with the less than one-tenth of one percent who refused to say whether they had ever married.

Table 6.3 gives the percentages of CAFN2 respondents who said "up to God" or "don't know" in answer to other questions about ideal family size. Nearly one-fifth for some questions and more than one-quarter for others said that the best number of children was "up to God": "She believes that one should not dictate to God the number of children one should bear" (CAFN2-fn: 0549). Asked what would be too many children for a woman to have, 28.9 percent refused to give a number—despite the fact that interviewers had been directed to "probe hard" for one.

Respondents often elaborated the concept "up to God." For example:

This man and his only wife . . . surely believe that man cannot decide for himself the number of children he is to have. Children come from God and things should be allowed to happen as it pleases God. They also believe that children can never be too

Table 6.3. Noncompliance of CAFN2 Respondents in
Number-Eliciting Questions

Question	"Up to God"	"Don't Know" or No Response	Total
Q.32a. If none would die, how many children is the best number to have?	18.5%	0.6%	19.1%
Q.32b. Where you live, how many children is the best number to have?	17.6	1.6	19.2
Q.38b. If you were poor, how many children would be best to have?	20.2	1.1	21.3
Q.38a. If you were very rich, how many children would you have?	21.4	0.6	22.0
Q.22. How many more children do you want?	24.6	1.9	26.5
Q.21. What do you think is the best number of children to have?	27.6	1.0	28.6
Q.30. How many is too many children for a woman to have?	20.7	8.2	28.9

many because if they are too many God will not allow . . . them
to [be] born. (CAFN2-fn: 0163)

One CAFN2 subject, as reported by his interviewer, summarized this
viewpoint:

The idea of God is dominant in his idea of family sizes. Definitely he does not want to discuss points which to him [are]
beyond our control. (CAFN2-fn: 2170)

Some subjects referred to divine punishment for assuming efficacy
with regard to procreation: "To him any attempt to limit the high

number of child bearing is to incur the anger of God" (CAFN1-fn: 0405). Others reaffirmed the traditional Yoruba religio-cultural doctrine of reincarnation:

> The respondent said her main problem is to get many more children and to see that those of her children that are dead are reborn into the family. (CAFN2-fn: 1450)

For a few, the care and education of children was "up to God" as well: "Her first aim is that God provides her with children, then to help her to take care of them" (CAFN2-fn: 1434). One insisted that the poor man with twelve children

> is blameless for not having the wherewithal to cater for the education of the children because children are God's gift to the man which he cannot reject. Even money to cater for the children is given by God, so the man may continue to look to God to provide. (CAFN2-sr: 2062)

Others expressed a similar view:

> Having many children should be a source of happiness. Children are God's blessing and gift to man. The man has only to pray that he may be able to cater for them and that they succeed in life. (CAFN2-sr: 2052)

> He believed that however poor a man is, he should have as many children as God gave him and should not stop having children on account of [absence of] wealth. His belief is that in spite of all hardships, the children would find their feet in life. (CAFN1-fn: 1205)

In fact, a substantial proportion of subjects balked at the Western concept of parental responsibility. Asked whether it was as easy to educate eight children as four and why, for instance, 16 percent answered that "it all depends" and another 7 percent said they didn't know or refused to respond at all. When these answers are considered together, nearly one-quarter of the sample refused to say that it is not as easy to educate eight children as four.

Restating the Yoruba Case

Many subjects, suspecting that the underlying values of the researchers favored small families for Yorubas, emphasized in defense
that they "find delight in having many children" (CAFN2-fn: 2253),
that a "large family is a blessing" (CAFN2-fn: 1421), that there is
"nothing bad in having a large family" (CAFN2-fn: 0354). Some qualified the point—"There is no sin in having many children if the parents can afford the expenses" (CAFN2-fn: 1734)—but others pointed
to "friends and acquaintances who had more than ten children and
who are not worse off" (CAFN2-fn: 1427).

For some, the questioning resulted in the reaffirmation that small
families are contrary to African ways: "He said that there is no good
thing in having no child. African society does not like the idea"
(CAFN2-fn: 2259); "He said that in African society one should marry
and have children whatever the number may be" (CAFN2-fn: 1919).
A farmer with one wife and five children, in answer to the question
about the best number of children, replied:

> This is a self-opinionated question. . . . The purpose of mar-
> riage is to have children, so it does not occur to me not to have
> more. . . . I have been visited by the family planning unit but do
> not find it good to continue the method.   (CAFN2-sr: 2160)

And another respondent

> gave a final conclusion that in case we are trying to know his
> impression on family planning he would like to tell us he is not
> interested in family planning. He said one should produce as
> [many children] as God provides. . . . He said there is no relation-
> ship between many children and poverty; all depends on destiny.
> (CAFN2-fn: 1417)

The Effect of Western Schooling on Compliance

Ability and willingness to comply with the interview process increased in direct proportion to the subjects' exposure to Western
education. We have seen the conflict between the demographers' re-

Table 6.4. Relation of Western Education Level to CAFN2 Respondents' Noncompliance in a Number-Eliciting Question by Highest Level of Western Education Reached

Western Education Level	"As Many as Possible"	"Up to God"	No Response	Total
None (N = 1,498)	13%	30%	7%	50%
1–4 years (N = 191)	10	13	8	31
5–6 years (N = 425)	7	12	9	29
Some secondary (N = 278)	8	10	9	27
Secondary certificate (N = 215)	7	8	11	26
Beyond secondary certificate (N = 389)	5	10	7	22

Note: Percentages calculated from responses to CAFN2 Question 30: Do you think a woman should have a lot of children? Is it possible to have too many? What would you say would be too many?

quirement for numbers and the reticence of some Yorubas to give those numbers. Therefore, one indicator of compliance was the ability and willingness to provide numbers in answer to questions requiring them. And for all questions requesting numerical answers, the proportion of respondents who supplied them correlated directly with their level of Western education.

For instance, Table 6.4 relates the percentages of respondents who answered "as many as possible" or "up to God" or gave no response at all to the question "Do you think a woman should have a lot of children? Is it possible to have too many? What would you say would be too many?" (CAFN2-Q.30) with the extent of their Western education. Researchers wanted numerical answers to the last part of the question. As the reader can see from the table, the highest level of schooling reached correlated inversely with proportions of respondents who refused to give numbers. Thirteen percent of those with no Western education answered "as many as possible," compared with just 5 percent of those who had more than a secondary school certificate. Thirty percent of subjects with no Western education replied "up to God," whereas just 10 percent with more than a secondary certificate did. Taken together, the proportion giving no number declined as their schooling increased: half the respondents with no Western education refused to give a number, compared with one-fifth (22 percent) of those who had gone beyond the secondary school certificate.

This correlation is hardly surprising. Western schools are practice grounds for categorizing oneself according to bureaucratic surveillance requirements. Students are expected to know their age and date of birth, for example. More important, schools teach students the value and practice of ranking themselves according to secondary roles within a bureaucratic organization.[4]

Conclusion

Regardless of how unbalanced resources may be in any encounter, dependent actors are not completely dependent or defenseless (Giddens, 1984: 32). Many subjects, particularly those who had not attended Western schools, resisted the lessons inherent in the CAFN questions. To resist Lesson 1, that the "real" family is the nuclear family, subjects argued that this notion was foreign to African society. In pointing to fosterage and the sibling educational chain, along with the foreign nature of the concept of conjugal relationship, respondents reaffirmed that the "real" family was the lineage.

Resisting Lesson 2, that children should be consciously evaluated according to a cost calculus, subjects not only balked at explicating children's rewards and costs but also raised such other considerations as community prestige and help in parents' old age. Many argued that they had to play the odds against child mortality or a child's potential for educational success. Resisting Lesson 3, that Western contraceptive methods are as morally acceptable as traditional measures, subjects argued that contraceptives were artifacts of foreign cultural imposition.

Many subjects simply refused to answer the questions deriving from the assumption inherent in Lesson 4, that personal efficacy is normal and natural. Between one-fifth and one-quarter asserted that fertility decisions were best left to God; some said that their children's care and education were "up to God" as well. In this way (and by elucidating the sibling educational chain) subjects refuted the efficacy-infused Western concept of parental responsibility. Resisting Lesson 5, that placing oneself under bureaucratic surveillance is normal and natural, subjects lied, evaded their questioners, refused to be questioned at all, or refused to respond to selected questions, sometimes by "making jest" or engaging in irrelevance and distraction.

Some subjects took the interview as an occasion to reaffirm traditional positions: "No pressure will make him cancel his belief that God gives children" (CAFN2-fn: 2170); "He made me to understand that he would continue child bearing [begetting] until he is not able to do so" (CAFN2-fn: 0423). They restated their case that large families are moral, necessary, and reasonable and that the number of children a person has and how those children are cared for is not a matter for personal decision-making or control.

These various forms of resistance are evidence that the Changing African Family—Nigeria projects were seen by many subjects as cultural imposition. As such, CAFN exemplifies world-system demography and raises important policy considerations.

7   The CAFN Projects
as Exercises in World-
System Demography
Policy Considerations

The authority of world-system demography to penetrate Nigeria and other Third World regions has been interpreted here as an extension of the right-to-invade that was militarily established during the historical period of European economic and cultural expansion. With contemporary times, this right-to-invade mandated the expansion of bureaucratic surveillance in these regions. Bureaucratic surveillance is disciplinary power—the stuff of social control.

As a bureaucratically organized, international, scientific effort funded by the Population Council and directed by Australian demographers—that is, an effort defined and controlled by elites within core nations—the Changing African Family–Nigeria projects (however well intentioned) proved to be exercises in world-system demography. CAFN drilled subjects and fieldworkers alike in compliance with bureaucratic surveillance, as opposed to family authority. By encouraging respondents to cooperate in *this* surveillance experience, the interviews legitimated and taught the value and practice of bureaucratic surveillance generally.

Subjects' compliance meant making themselves available to other First World lessons as well. Respondents heard that the "real" family is nuclear, that children should be consciously evaluated according to

96

a cost calculus, that Western contraceptive methods are morally acceptable, and that attitudes and behaviors of personal efficacy are normal and natural. Together these lessons schooled subjects in values and beliefs supporting purposefully limited family size.

Many Yoruba subjects resisted, some by lying and tricking interviewers, others by confronting fieldworkers more directly, insisting that assumptions underlying the research were foreign to African society. They had no reason to use contraceptive devices, the latter argued, because they found nothing wrong in having many children. In fact, they said, God is in charge, and children are God's ultimate blessing. This kind of resistance is evidence that the CAFN projects were seen by many respondents as cultural impositions.

The empirical generalization that CAFN was an exercise in cultural imposition leads to important policy considerations for demographic research. The first and most apparent consideration raised by this analysis involves First World scientists' disregard for respondents' privacy, or "territorial selves," coupled with the potential de- and reconstruction of indigenous cultures without concern for unforeseen, possibly negative consequences. A second consideration, raised less directly by this analysis, involves the extent to which demographic inquiry is determined by the agendas of its major funding agencies. Taken together, these issues suggest a broad policy question: how might demographers continue international inquiry while at the same time respecting their subjects? Put another way, how might international demography open doors between the First and Third Worlds, rather than export the Weberian "iron cage" of bureaucratic surveillance?

Despite the fact that I have analyzed research undertaken in the 1970s to raise these questions, they are neither dated nor isolated issues. From the Knowledge, Attitude, and Practice (KAP) surveys in the 1960s to the World Fertility Survey (WFS) in the 1970s and early 1980s to the current Demographic and Health Surveys (DHS), large-scale fertility survey projects have penetrated the Third World. Asking about birth control needs and practices, these projects have carried lessons similar to those inherent in CAFN. Moreover, the major funding agencies remain in core nations and persist in driving the field.[1] We turn now to the questions of subject exploitation and research reactivity.

Exploitation and Reactivity

My evidence suggests that the Changing African Family–Nigeria projects exploited their subjects by pursuing the primary aim of the research—to gather data—even when doing so went against respondents' wishes, constituted culturally aggressive invasion of subjects' privacy, and disregarded their beliefs. Traditionally in Yorubaland, for instance, reincarnation into one's own clan is believed to be the ultimate reward for a good life (Bascom, 1969: 75–76). A personal name such as "Father Returns" or "Mother Returns" is given to a child of the same sex as the ancestor he or she is believed to reincarnate (Fadipe, 1970: 261–300; Bascom, 1969: 70–71). Therefore, to limit one's progeny is to deny deserving ancestors rebirth (Caldwell and Caldwell, 1987: 416). Further, to die without children stifles one's own opportunity for reincarnation (Caldwell, 1976a: 206–7).

Even among Yorubas who no longer hold these traditional beliefs, limiting family size—or even so much as stating that intention—is generally abhorred as sinful (Caldwell and Caldwell, 1987: 412–13; see also Caldwell and Caldwell, 1978). Many respondents said they could not reveal the number of children they wanted because it was against their religion to do so, and they feared retribution:

> She felt if she answered the question how many children one should have clearly, she might have repercussions, as she has not given any birth to any baby.   (CAFN2-fn: 1151)

> She is scared to give the number of children she wants because she fears . . . that God may kill all the ones she has if she does that.   (CAFN2-fn: 1234)

Nevertheless, interviewers were directed to elicit specific numbers from all subjects. On the questionnaire form, categories such as "up to God," and "no answer" were followed in parentheses by the directive "But probe hard for a number." And some interviewers proved adept at eliciting those numbers, even to the point of badgering subjects. As one explained, the respondent "kept saying 'up to God'—to which I said, 'If god asked you to choose, what would you choose?' " The need for numerical data blinded researchers to the exploitation inherent in gathering it.

My evidence further suggests that CAFN was reactive. According to interviewers, one subject "said that the questions can guide a man on how to plan his family" (CAFN3-fn: 0282); another "expressed several times that he considered the questions to be educative, especially the ones that reminded him of family planning" (CAFN2-fn: 0983). In providing such "guidance" and "education," the CAFN projects implicitly challenged indigenous local norms and behavior—without regard for potential negative consequences. The language of the questions subtly encouraged the control of fertility by means of imported contraceptives and carried the lesson that the "real" family is nuclear—even though respondents had asserted, and the Caldwells themselves have acknowledged, that high fertility is rational and functional for large portions of Third World parents (Caldwell, 1976a, 1982b). To understand why, we need to recognize such factors as high infant and child mortality rates, the fact that wealth flow in much of the Third World continues to move upward, and the impact of nucleation on societies organized around the extended family.

Persistent High Infant Mortality

As we saw in Chapter 1, the infant mortality rate in Yorubaland (as in much of the Third World) is strikingly high. Findings from the 1990 Nigeria Demographic and Health Survey indicate that nearly one in five children dies before age five ("Nigeria DHS Survey," 1992: 2). Thirty-three percent of the Caldwells' CAFN2 sample had lost at least one child: 9 percent had lost two children; 8 percent had lost three or four; 3 percent had lost five or six; another 3 percent, seven or more children (one respondent reported having lost thirty offspring). A significantly higher proportion of Yorubas generally than of the interview sample can expect to experience the loss of at least one child during the course of their parenting career (see Uhlenberg, 1980).

Because several (or all) of a parent's children may die, many Yorubas consider any effort to limit family size irresponsible (Caldwell and Caldwell, 1987: 412). Over the last two decades demographers and epidemiologists have become increasingly concerned about Third World infant and child mortality. But until increasing concern is matched by decreasing mortality rates, the question needs to be debated—earnestly and in plain public view—whether it is ethical to discourage high fertility in areas where infant and child mortality remains so fearsome.

Upward Wealth Flow

A second reason that high fertility is rational throughout much of the Third World involves intergenerational wealth flow. Upward wealth flow remains very much the reality among Yorubas (Caldwell and Caldwell, 1987: 421). In fact, children work for their parents throughout the entire life cycle, providing

> physical work as children; presents, money and physical assistance as adults; help on the farm or in trading as parents age; and more complete help with approaching infirmity; finally the appropriate services for the dead. . . . This is still true even in most urban middle-class homes, where assistance from adult children to parents may be very substantial now that adult children can earn high salaries.   (Caldwell and Caldwell, 1976: 360)

In nations where there is little or no provision for any equivalent of social security in old age or where parents need children's help to accommodate subsistence-level survival, the question arises whether demographers ought rightly to be involved in persuading these parents to have fewer children. Put another way, with high fertility economically advantageous and perhaps even necessary to survival for countless Third World parents, surely demographers should conscientiously debate the ethics of discouraging it.

Nuclear versus Extended Families

The Caldwells stress that family nucleation (emotional and economic withdrawal of a monogamous couple and their children from the surrounding kin network) is necessary to fertility decline (Caldwell, 1976a, 1977a, 1982b; Caldwell and Caldwell, 1978, 1987: 430).[2] Many having first been encouraged by colonialism (Caldwell, Orubu- loye, and Caldwell, 1991), Third World families will increasingly become nucleated, according to the Caldwells, as a result of cultural transmission from the West. For the most part this will occur through Western education, along with media penetration (Caldwell, 1977a, 1980, 1982b; Caldwell and Caldwell, 1978). But international demo- graphic research as well has the potential to promote this form of Westernization. As we have seen, one lesson inherent in CAFN was that the "real" family is nuclear, its cohesion rooted in the spousal relationship.

World-system demography generally ignores the potential conse- quences of culturally imposed nucleation. Yet demographers might well argue whether it is appropriate to encourage nucleation in parts of the Third World where the nuclear family, a cultural imposition, may not function effectively. As discussed in Chapter 5, Yoruba chil- dren traditionally belong to the lineage as much as to any particular mother. Many adults, not just biological parents, are responsible for children's upbringing. Apparently this system worked well in tra- ditional Yorubaland, and it has been adapted to more recent child- rearing needs. There is, for example, a "sibling educational chain" among Yorubas, whereby older educated children within the ex- tended family facilitate younger siblings' education (Caldwell, 1976a: 221).

Meanwhile, there is evidence that nucleation (at least as it has oc- curred in East Africa; see Kilbride and Kilbride, 1990) can put new strain on family life and decrease the perceived value of children, one result being more frequent occurrences of child abuse and neglect. Then, too, as relationship-cohesive couples appear to find it increas- ingly problematic to rear children together, even in societies where the nuclear family is regarded as the norm (of the 20 percent of U.S. children living below the poverty line, most are in female-headed, single-parent homes), one must wonder whether it is responsible to promote the nuclear family as a functional alternative to the extended kin model.

In sum, demographers, recognizing that their research is hardly nonreactive, should resolutely debate the supposed rewards (and for whom, primarily) against potential costs (and for whom, primarily) of Third World cultural de- and reconstruction. The refuting argument typically made here is that Third World respondents are not passive but active participants in research and are not blindly led by First World researchers. I am not suggesting that Third World respondents are merely passive receptors of First World cultural aggression; indeed, I have presented evidence of respondent resistance. I am arguing that if greater money and power allow First World demographers to be of any influence (and I think this is the case), then we need to ponder the potential effects of that influence.

And it would not hurt us to consider our motives as well. When President Lyndon Johnson first asked Congress for fertility control funds, he did so on the grounds that high population growth rates in the Third World "challenge our own security" (quoted in Hodgson, 1988: 549). Bertrand Russell had observed in 1929: "It cannot be expected that the most powerful military nations will sit still while other nations reverse the balance of power by the mere process of breeding" (1985: 161; see also Thompson, 1929).[3]

World-System Demography and Funding Agencies

The question of motives raises the second policy consideration: to what extent demographic inquiry is directed and limited by the core agencies that fund it. Paul Demeny, 1986 president of the Population Association of America, has argued that demographers' reliance on large-scale funding has made the "official population sector" virtually their only patron. And funders require "with remarkable consistency" that research proceed from "the received population policy line" (Demeny, 1988: 464; see also McNicoll, 1988: 13).

Headquartered in New York, the Population Council, CAFN's funding agency, was established in 1952 by John D. Rockefeller III as an organizational aid to the emerging global birth-control movement (see Demerath, 1976; Hartmann, 1987; Shapiro, 1985: esp. chap. 3). Initially, he funded the council personally. Eventually the Rockefeller and Ford foundations, along with the United States Agency for International Development (USAID, or AID), the World Bank, and the United Nations Fund for Population Activities (UNFPA) funneled monies to the council (Caldwell, 1988a; Caldwell and Caldwell, 1986; Notestein 1982).[4]

From its inception the Population Council has played a key role in the design and implementation of family planning programs. After World War II, demographers increasingly agreed that Third World population growth had become a "problem" and that high fertility was having dire consequences.[5] What developed was the thoroughly institutionalized "family planning establishment" (Demerath, 1976: 34) that largely defines world-system demography today. As demographers consistently failed to question global wealth distribution, the need to limit Third World fertility became demographic orthodoxy (see Crane and Finkle 1989; Demeny 1986; Hodgson 1988).[6] Even though this line of argument lost momentum during the 1980s, Third World overpopulation continues to be a strong "demon" in demographic literature (e.g., Grebnik, 1989).

By 1967, Caldwell had affiliated with the Population Council as African Regional Director in Demography, an affiliation that continued through the CAFN research and beyond, despite his "being an outspoken skeptic of the 'family planning' solution to rapid population growth" (Schultz, 1983: 162).[7] Unable to venture a project of the Changing African Family's magnitude without major funding, he "convinced the people at the Population Council that they needed African data" (personal communication), whereupon the council provided funding and an adviser. Critical sociologists of science would argue that affiliation with the Population Council must have constrained the researchers' scientific freedom. But Caldwell has prepared an answer: "This accusation, which has been common enough, appears . . . to have underestimated academics' ability to describe their aims in ways sufficiently close to the needs of the funders while continuing to do very much what they want" (Caldwell, 1988a: 15).

With regard to CAFN, principal researchers did describe the project's aims in ways sufficiently close to the needs of the Population Council. At the onset, Field Director Helen Ware drafted a letter to prospective participating professors, (Appendix B, #10). The aim of the research, she explained, was to examine societal changes which might lead Third World peoples "to a new awareness of the costs and benefits of children." The emphasis would be upon "the point of transition, when women first begin salaried employment, when modern contraception becomes available in an area and when other changes occur."

In promising to focus on children's costs and benefits at a point of transition, Ware assured CAFN funders that the project was to be in keeping with mainstream demographic theory. Her language proceeds from the "new home economics" model (see, e.g., Becker, 1960, 1965) at the micro level and from demographic transition theory at the macro level. Demographic transition theory is demography's counterpart to the Parsonian functionalist-evolutionary or modernization paradigm (which defined social science in the 1950s, when demography emerged as a full-fledged discipline) whereby societies "unfold" (Giddens, 1987: 28) or evolve according to the principle of "adaptive upgrading" (Parsons, 1951, 1966).[8]

The language of the CAFN funding proposal promised mainstream demographic research; at the same time, Caldwell apparently did do very much what he wanted in CAFN. Generally, he amassed considerable new evidence to support his case that high fertility in the Third World was reasonable. Nevertheless, if scientific freedom means considering the range of all possible paradigms, foundation-funded scholars "are by no means as free as they may often assume" (Sjoberg and Nett, 1968: 120). Once Caldwell had posited Third World fertility behavior as reasonable, a logical next step would have been to investigate structural causes. But structural or contextual variables were conspicuously absent. As is true of survey research generally, CAFN questionnaires presented hypothetical financial and health difficulties as respondents' personal problems, not as public issues (cf. Mills, 1959).

Some respondents did raise structurally embedded concerns. They voiced needs for more equal access to formal education; better medical care, especially to combat infertility and child mortality; expanded employment opportunities and more money. But fieldworkers were likely to dismiss such issues. As one reported, "She demanded to know if the government was prepared to help her, but I explained the purpose of the subject to her" (CAFN2-fn: 1295). Another interviewer consistently described complaints and requests as "rascality": "He gives signs of some sort of rascality. He brags and talk too much of the fact that money is not equally distributed in the country" (CAFN2-fn: 0557). As well-trained scientific experts, indigenous fieldworkers for the most part recognized only that "system of problems" established within their discipline (Schutz, 1970: 242, 259–60).

Moreover, questions that might have been derived from other than the mainstream demographic paradigm (such as world-system theory, for example) were not raised, even though Caldwell himself has recognized and even pointed to international power disparities as important in global social change. He has argued, for example, that demographers' "omitting transmitted European cultural traditions from the study of modernization" has been an "almost incredible feat. It is like leaving Hellenization out of an examination of social change in the fifth century B.C. Macedonia or leaving Roman social influences out of a treatise on Britain in the second century A.D." (Caldwell, 1982b: 148). Indeed, he has said that "the central fact of our times has been the ability of the dominant Western economy to establish a global economy and society. . . . The export of its social arrangements has . . . been based on . . . the ability of the paramount exporting economy to sell its society as well" (1981b: 20). A comparison of these published opinions with the CAFN procedures would seem to indicate that the directors' reliance on and participation in what I have called world-system demography influenced the projects paradigmatically.

Demographers need to debate—again, earnestly and in plain public view—what effects, if any, their funding has on their research. According to Demeny, international demography "seeks, and with the power of the purse enforces, predictability, control, and subservience." Practitioners' readiness to play "the roles of reliable messenger of orthodoxy and expert technician" reflects "the success of bureaucratic control over social science activity of all stripes" (Demeny, 1988: pp. 471, 474). Demographers ought to explore alternative funding sources and consider relatively small, less expensive projects. In this way, demography might encourage more truly indigenous research—research conceived, directed, and funded regionally or locally throughout the Third World. The promotion of indigenous-controlled research internationally might thus become a priority, which has not been the case (Demeny, 1988: 474).

This last point raises a tangentially related question: To what extent does the discipline primarily educate Third World demographers to play the roles of "reliable messenger of orthodoxy and expert technician"? It is no secret (although it is seldom publicly spoken of) that international sciences and multinational corporations have generated an international, core-directed "semiaristocracy" of Westernized indigenous elites, privileged in comparison with the proletarianized masses (Amin, 1976; see also Bradshaw, 1988; Nolan and Lenski, 1985; Wimberly, 1990). Third World demographers, dependent on core-controlled agencies, educational institutions, and journals for their credentials and publishing, have little choice but to adhere (publicly at least) to the orthodox "party line" of world-system demography. One result can be that an "elitist ideology" is "grafted onto" dependence, and a peripheral nation's national culture and autonomy degenerates (Amin, 1976: 211–14).

Demography needs to consider whether its own Third World indigenous elites are socialized and credentialed—as were the CAFN fieldworkers—to act as regimented First World–Third World go-betweens. Are we teaching graduate students technical proficiencies while ignoring the structural and cultural context of demographic variables in their own home countries? How might the discipline's graduate students be better educated as persons capable of framing problems, gathering and analyzing data, writing and eventually publishing with an indigenous voice?

Opening Doors

These issues, taken together, suggest the broader question of how we might engage in international science and still respect the cultural integrity of Third World subjects. How can demography be effective in opening doors of legitimate communication between First and Third World peoples? How can international demography do more to advance the cause of humanist, reflexive change in the twenty-first century and be less a tool for unexamined bureaucratic surveillance in the cause of First World interests?

This is a big question. World-system demography hesitates to ask it. Indeed, its interventionist heritage and major methodological paradigm resist such questions. Over the past five decades demography has exemplified what Thomas S. Kuhn termed "normal science": practitioners have shared a taken-for-granted world view; articulating the modernization–intervention theoretical paradigm, demographic research has been highly technified "mop-up work" (1970: 24). With technical precision its mark of excellence, a field interests itself in "puzzle-solving" (Kuhn, 1970: 35) or "nuts and bolts" (Hodgson, 1983: 27) questions to the exclusion of ethical ones (see also Redner, 1987).[9] Geoffrey McNicoll has bemoaned the "occupational characteristic of demographers" that leads them "to tolerate, and by their attentions worsen, the imbalance between demographic precision and detail on the one hand and casualness of treatment of nondemographic contextual and policy variables on the other" (1988: 20).[10]

Despite all this, there is precedent for policy debate among demographers.[11] Third World delegates to the first international World Population Conference, which met at Bucharest in 1974, introduced unequal wealth distribution as an independent variable in population growth issues and proposed distributive justice, or global redistribution of wealth and power, as a remedy. Within world-system demography "the effort hardly outlived the conference" (McNicoll, 1988: 15); nevertheless, the challenge at Bucharest moved the modernization–intervention paradigm from taken-for-granted "truth" to debatable ideology.

Since then a few demographers (e.g., Greenhalgh, 1990; Johansson, 1991; Levine, 1986; Mason, 1992; Stonich, 1989) have proposed that the discipline consider historical, cultural, structural-contextual, or political economy variables in analyses. For instance, in a working paper published by the Population Council, Susan Greenhalgh, senior associate in the council's Center for Policy Studies, suggested a "new analytic perspective": one that directs attention to the embeddedness of community institutions in structures and processes—especially political and economic ones—operating at regional, national, and global levels, and to the historical roots of those macro–micro linkages (1990: 5–6). Susan S. Stonich, writing in *Population and Development Review* the previous year, had used a world-system perspective to examine the environmental consequences of population growth in Honduras. Among her conclusions:

> [T]he ways in which natural resources have been exploited have been greatly shaped by the dictates of capitalist accumulation. . . . Although the rapid increase in population growth in the region is a matter for serious concern, population growth per se cannot adequately explain the destructive land-use patterns that have emerged in the south.   (1989: 289–90)

This emergent "trickle" (Greenhalgh 1990: 22) of theoretical innovation is promising. More dramatically, it is time to entertain the suggestion that there are powerful ways of knowing other than the Euro-linear view that seeks ultimately to predict and control. Molefi Kete Asante has brought a world-system perspective to international culture with the concept "rhetoric of domination." For Asante, paradigms "rooted in Eurocentric viewpoints" dominate global rhetoric. Such rhetoric has three characteristics: definitional control over a rhetorical territory, required credentials for those allowed that control, and the stifling of opposing dialogue (1987: 27–29).

World-system demography both effects and reflects such rhetorical domination. Practitioners of an alternative scientific paradigm might strive instead for cooperative interpretation and understanding. Here rhetoric would become "the productive thrust of language into the unknown in an attempt to create harmony and balance in the midst of disharmony and indecision" (Asante, 1987: 35). Asante is suggesting a redistribution of global rhetorical power so that First World–Third World social scientific interaction might be less an exercise in bureaucratic surveillance and more an occasion for the powerful simply to listen. Some of this may be beginning to happen in demography. The Caldwells' own, and their students', anthropological approach (Caldwell and Caldwell, 1988c; Caldwell, Hill, and Hull, 1984; see Appendix A) is hopeful (see also Greenhalgh, 1990). The Mellon Foundation is currently interested in funding more anthropological research. The growing acceptance of focus groups in international demographic research is another positive sign.

Conclusion

Reflecting the social conditions in which they were produced, the Changing African Family–Nigeria research documents allowed me to examine a dialectical process in the social reconstruction of reality in Yorubaland. The dialectic was played out by First World scientists interacting with Third World subjects. The researcher–respondent interaction under analysis in this study reflected core–periphery encounters within world-system demography.

My analysis assumes that social science research is interactive and represents the sociocultural milieu, replete with power relationships, in which it is found. Because global stratification is ideational or cultural, as well as economic, exploitation is not only structural but cultural and is present in global scientific research, including world-system demography.

Value changes within peripheral societies are not indications simply of *cultural diffusion* but the results of core-controlled *cultural imposition*. If international science is an agent of global rhetorical domination, world-system demography brings that domination to the arena of Third World fertility. Small-family values are Western cultural impositions. One agent in their imposition is world-system demography, which often employs Westernized indigenous elites as fieldworkers—as First World culture-carriers.

Four persistent themes characterizing the history of Nigeria since its earliest colonialism have informed my findings: (1) Eurocentric devaluation of the Yoruba; (2) the de- and reconstruction of Yoruba social structure, culture, and economy; (3) the external orchestration of change in Yorubaland via bureaucratic surveillance; and (4) indigenous resistance to foreign penetration. CAFN followed the colonial legacy of invasion and the removal of Third World resources (data) with little regard for the suppliers (subjects). Core funded and influenced, CAFN was one agent in the export of bureaucratic surveillance. The projects were both culturally aggressive and paradigmatically limited. Professionally credentialed researchers claimed definitional control over a rhetorical territory. Furthermore, they claimed authority to direct interviewer–respondent interaction. Subjects were expected to respond efficiently: to answer only the questions put. Conversation defined as irrelevant was either discouraged or dismissed.

Respondents who found the research intrusive recognized it as an exercise in the rhetoric of domination. With intervention a major factor in the heritage of world-system demography, it is hardly surprising that demographers have been slow to consider issues of research reactivity or to question whether their research in the Third World is culturally aggressive. Moreover, the major research paradigm of world-system demography discourages asking policy questions. Nevertheless, with some evidence of theoretical and methodological debate and nascent change within international demography, it seems appropriate to ask whether a new paradigm can emerge that will seriously challenge the present one.

To open doors to the Third World, social scientists might listen for the purpose of understanding, rather than simply survey for the purpose of prediction and control. If such a shift were achieved, Third World social scientific research might no longer be considered (as one CAFN fieldworker summarized his reticent subjects' objections) "another elitist ruse." Demeny has called for funders' "conscious and deliberate" allocation of monies "for independent and rigorous scientific inquiry" and for the "critical examination" of alternative policy approaches with regard to Third World fertility (1988: 465). Perhaps some of that money will be forthcoming.

Appendixes
Notes
Bibliography
Index

Appendix A
The Study
Design

This study was designed to generate grounded theory by qualitatively analyzing documents from the Changing African Family–Nigeria projects.

The CAFN projects yielded both quantitative and qualitative data. The quantitative data consisted of coded responses to the face-to-face, structured interview questions. These data were available in bound marginals (frequency distributions of grouped data) for each project and on computer tapes prepared for statistical analysis. In addition, they have been heavily reported by Caldwell and others (e.g., Caldwell, 1976b, 1977a, 1979a, 1979b, 1981a, 1981c; Caldwell and Caldwell, 1976, 1977, 1981a, 1981b, 1985, 1987; Caldwell and Ware, 1977; Okediji et al., 1976; Ware, 1975, 1978). I accepted and made use of the findings put forth in those publications. Although I used the quantitative data to run some cross-tabulations, primarily I worked with the documents and qualitative data, which are described below and in Appendix B.

Generating Grounded Theory

Generating grounded theory involves the "discovery of theory from data" (Glaser and Strauss, 1967: 1). The researcher develops empirical generalizations and theoretical propositions while "in intimate relationship with the data" (Strauss, 1987: 6). John C. Caldwell's own approach to

113

demographic investigation is of this nature. Terming it "anthropological methodology" or the "micro-approach to demographic inquiry" (Caldwell and Caldwell, 1988b; Caldwell, Hill, and Hull, 1984), he explains:

> Primarily, this means a continuing and developing insight based upon the local residence of the principal investigator or investigators. . . . The central participation of the principal investigator in all parts of the work is a necessity because the anthropological approach is fundamentally based on the construction of hypotheses and their subsequent confirmation or rejection. This is a continuing intellectual process.   (Caldwell and Caldwell, 1988b: 5)

That Caldwell kept the wealth of documents described here and in Appendix B is evidence of his seeing the research process as developing and ongoing.

Developing grounded theory involves induction, deduction, verification, and integration. From the data the researcher discovers conceptual categories and their properties, along with generative hypotheses, or "generalized relations among the categories and their properties" (Glaser and Strauss, 1967: 35). Subsequent steps are verification and theoretical integration. There is chronological order in these processes, but at the same time they blend and overlap.

Integral to generating grounded theory is coding, or conceptually breaking the data into a multiplicity of categories, properties, and relationships. Beginning with the CAFN1 Block Reports (see Appendix B, #1), I scrutinized the documents one sentence at a time, writing down impressions, reactions, and ideas about behaviors, values, and beliefs apparent there. Initially, my coding was "open" or unrestricted, the goal being to "open up" inquiry (cf. Strauss, 1987: 29).

Gradually, coding incorporated dimensionalizing, or making distinctions with attention to variance. For instance, the emergent category "respondents' receptivity to being interviewed" illustrated wide variance, as evidenced by these two examples:

> Block 76
> Interviewer: Oluremi Alese
> When I was first given the block I don't know exactly where it is or how the people would welcome me. I looked at the area and the following day went to the first house. I explained what I had come for and the woman was very nice. She told me everything about

herself, and that she had used contraceptives. She even offered me some *Amala* [yam flour cakes] with about four pieces of meat.

The following day I was warmly welcomed again, as the women were expecting me.

Block 51
Interviewer: Olanike Awolowo
When I got to the block some of the women thought I had come to ask some important questions, so many of them ran away from me. But on explaining further some of them answered. . . .
Some were not willing to tell me the number of their children. . . .
Many of them also promised to answer if I returned in the evening, but on getting there they would not answer until the next day.

As time went on, my coding progressed to noting causal conditions and consequences associated with emergent concepts. For example, field-workers consistently equated subjects' receptivity to being interviewed with literacy or education. Noting such relationships between concepts occurred simultaneously with developing generative hypotheses.

Generative hypotheses are provisional and designed to be interrelated, altered, perhaps discarded. They are meant to precipitate further questions and hypothetical relationships. They "stimulate the line of investigation in profitable directions" (Strauss, 1987: 21).

After several weeks of coding, I made the following notes, reproduced here as they appeared in my notebook under the heading *Themes fr the data:*

1. Hi fert. is desirable amg. the Yoruba
2. Opp costs for women don't exist?
3. Communal child-rearing lowers costs
4. The survey itself is an agent for change, becomes an educating/resocializing tool.
5. Resistance to family planning programs

These notes could be understood as generative hypotheses. As I proceeded, my task was to ascertain whether the data continued to support them. Here I put various questions to the data. What was actually happening in the data? What were the basic problems faced by the participants? What accounted for these problems? What category or property of a category, or what part of my emerging theory, did an incident indicate—

or refute? Questions like these "tend to force" (Strauss, 1987: 30) the generation of core theoretical concepts.

With the exception of my central concept, world-system demography, my core concepts—bureaucratic surveillance, dialectic of control, performance teams, cultural capital—could be understood at the beginning as "sensitizing" concepts. Drawn from sociological theory, they provided "a general sense of reference and guidance" but not "prescriptions of what to see" (Blumer, 1969: 148). While I came to this project familiar with these concepts, I reread and studied them as I analyzed the data. The process was one of ongoing "sensitizing" while at the same time the data provided empirical support for my core concepts. These concepts, then, developed within the context of my data.

The next step was verification, based on theoretical sampling: systematic, "selective coding" around each core concept while meticulously searching new data and returning to previously coded data for contrary evidence (Strauss, 1987: 33, 51–58). Here I played devil's advocate, looking to prove the theory wrong or to find empirically indicated modifications.

For example, in an initial coding of the CAFN1 Block Reports early in my analysis, I found widespread subject resistance to being interviewed. Subsequent coding of CAFN2 and CAFN3 data suggested less reticence among Western-educated subjects. Upon returning to the CAFN1 Block Reports for a second coding, I found the same negative correlation between Western education and resistance. I consequently modified my emergent theory to incorporate this later finding. I continued this process of modification with regard to all the data. Eventually I reached the point of "theoretical saturation" (Glaser and Strauss, 1967: 61), when additional analysis no longer contributed to my discovering anything new.

The final step in grounded theory generation is theoretical integration, "the ever-increasing organization or articulation of the components of the theory" (Strauss, 1987: 21). This proceeded systematically throughout the analysis, at least partly by means of writing theoretical memos and drawing theoretically integrative diagrams. Theoretical integration also took place during the writing of the monograph, even through the final draft.

The CAFN Documents

The qualitative data in the documents can be classified in seven categories:

1. the interview schedules;
2. responses to open-ended questions;
3. interviewers' training manuals;
4. forms to be completed by fieldworkers;
5. supervisory and explanatory memos to fieldworkers;
6. accounts of field experiences written by interviewers and supervisors;
7. editors' remarks on the accuracy of recorded responses.

The documents were (and still are) available in bound volumes in the library of the Department of Demography, Research School of Social Sciences, Australian National University, and also in the department's archives. Some examples from the foregoing categories follow. A more detailed listing appears in Appendix B.

The Interview Schedules

The schedules began by requiring the interviewer to record the questionnaire number and date, the interviewer number, and the language in which the interview was conducted (English, Yoruba, or both). Schedules contained structured, semistructured precoded, and unstructured open-ended questions.

Most structured questions asked for demographic data, such as age, religion, occupation, education, and marital status. Others, designed to yield independent variables, inquired about such facts as whether the respondent had ever been to a hospital or had consulted a Western doctor.

Semistructured precoded questions, employed primarily in CAFN1, were designed to allow respondents to answer in their own words but were followed by precoded response categories that had been developed through extensive dialogue with Yoruba staff and other informants and were modified during early days in the field (see Appendix B, #4 and #12). Response categories were not meant to be read to subjects, although at times this probably occurred. Question 7a, CAFN1, designed to yield data regarding sexual abstinence practices, is an example of a semistructured question with its precoded responses.

Do you think that a woman ought to live apart from her husband
for a period after she has given birth to a child? (This does not mean
living in separate parts of the same compound.) Or should she live
with him but abstain from sexual relations? Or what?
1. She should live apart.
2. She should live with him but *abstain*.
3. It's up to her, she should choose.
4. Only if she doesn't want another baby right away.
5. There is no reason to live apart or abstain for a long period.
6. Other (specify)

Unstructured open-ended questions allowed subjects to answer in
their own words, and no precoded response categories followed. But the
responses to most of the questions were expected to be relatively short;
only two or three lines were provided for the interviewer to record each
answer, preceded by the instruction "Write in (coding to be supplied
later)." The following four examples appeared in the CAFN2 schedule:

Q.35. If you won the lottery and won an enormous amount of
money (say ₦20,000 or £10,000), what would you do with it?

Q.36a. What job or position would you most like to have (or, for the
oldest group, have had)?

Q.36b. What job or position would you most like one of your sons
to have?

Q.36c. What job or position would you most like one of your
daughters to have?

In addition to short-answer questions, four unstructured CAFN2 questions were designed to encourage the respondent to talk freely, and a full
blank page followed each one so that the response could be recorded in
full. Questions 14 through 17 in CAFN1 Part B, were also of this type
(see Appendix B, #40). Question 17, for example, read as follows:

When you first used family planning, how did you bring yourself
to be able to do it? Were you surprised that you could act this
way? What happened at that time? Just how did you come to make
the jump?

Responses to Open-ended Questions

Answers to unstructured CAFN1 Questions 14–17 ranged in length from several paragraphs to one sentence. Here is one answer to Question 14, which asked when and why the respondent first thought about family planning:

> *#0438:* I thought about it 10 years ago when I had an abortion by myself. I was pregnant by my husband's brother and I did not want my husband to know about it. So I aborted it. It was after the abortion that I went to a native doctor for some preventive medicine. He gave me a ring which I use when I want to have sex.

And two responses to Question 17, quoted above:

> *#0001.* Nothing happened.
> *#0002.* I started practicing rhythm in 1971. I was surprised that I could act this way because if my fiance did not force me I couldn't have done it.

For examples of verbatim responses to open-ended, short-answer questions, see Appendix B, #42–45 (CAFN2) and #49, 51, 52 (CAFN3).

Interviewer's Training Manuals

Each project's "Interviewer's Manual" was an eight- to ten-page typed, single-spaced booklet of instructions for determining who should be interviewed and how, detailed explanations of the questions, and directives for assigning the responses to semistructured precoded questions (see Appendix B, #4, 33). Here, for example, is the explanation of a CAFN2 question:

> *Page 13* [of interview schedule] Question 18(b)(i)
> Means, leaving the costs of education aside, do you actually spend more money on all of your children than you would if you had more children? Possible examples are that the parents insure the health of [their] children, buy them bicycles, give them holidays, and better clothes which they would not give to ten children so that whereas the total cost (excluding education) of 4 children is ₦1,000 a year, the total cost of 10 children would only have been ₦800.

Forms to Be Completed by Fieldworkers

The data include many forms, designed to be completed by editors, field supervisors, and interviewers (see Appendix B, #17–21 and 26–31 for examples).

Supervisory and Explanatory Memos to Fieldworkers

Supervisory memos had to do with work practices, and explanatory memos dealt with problem areas in the field (see Appendix B, #15).

Here is an example of a *supervisory memo* from CAFN1; it is signed by Pat Caldwell:

IMPORTANT

Unless all interviewers have had satisfactory check with supervisors regarding no. of children living and dead and also question 13 checked out, we will not keep them on after Wednesday.

They must have satisfactory maps that they can use themselves. Each woman interviewed must be able to be found again.

For an example of an *explanatory memo,* see Appendix B, #5.

*Accounts of Field Experiences Written by
Interviewers and Supervisors*

This category comprises written comments recounting experiences in the field and directed upward to the research directors.

Interviewers' accounts appeared in several forms. In both CAFN2 and CAFN3, a blank page marked "Final Notes" was attached to each questionnaire; interviewers were expected to write in their comments regarding the interview. For CAFN2 this procedure resulted in "Final Notes" (see Appendix B, #46); for CAFN3 the resulting data were collected as "Comments from Final Page of Questionnaires, Project 3" (see Appendix B, #50). Additional sources of interviewers' accounts were their "Daily Reports of Interviewing at Centers" from CAFN2 (see Appendix B, #41), and the eighty-five "Block Reports" written by CAFN1 interviewers after their first ten days in the field (see Appendix B, #1).

Supervisors' accounts are found also in the CAFN1 Block Reports. Two examples follow:

Block No. 13
Block No. 14
Interviewer: Helen Adetiloye (Supervisor)
I went with Tayo Ayoade to her block at Iralende on 25th May to supervise her.
The area is a fairly vast one. We visited some of the respondents

who did only Part A. We tried to put them at ease and re-interview them. They insisted that they were telling the truth when they said they had never used contraceptives.

The interviewer did her work well.

Block No. 18

Interviewer: Abiola Ososanya (Supervisor)

I went out with Miss Mojisola Otukoya, interviewer no. 75, in Yemetu Aladorin Area. The area is directly behind St. Michael's Secondary Modern School.

There are only eight houses on the block. The area is a remote area, most of the women there are illiterates. They still believe in the traditional way i.e. abstaining for two-three years after giving birth to a child. Six of the women are from the Eastern States.

We explained our mission to the first woman in the first house, and she only did part A. We had some jokes with her so that we could get more facts from her, but she said that she told the truth the first time she was interviewed. I told her that not only women who use pills or went to the clinic for I.U.D. are practising family planning. I explained the rhythm and withdrawal methods to her, asked whether she has practised it, but she said she has not heard anything about it.

We entered seven houses like that, but none of them did part B. The women said that Miss Otukoya has explained everything to them clearly and that they have told her the truth. There was no-body to interview again in that block, because she said that she had finished with the block yesterday.

Judging from what I saw, Miss Otukoya is a good interviewer, because she asked the women about the second part intelligently and clearly.

Editors' Remarks on the Accuracy of Recorded Responses

One example of an editor's written remarks concerning the accuracy of responses as recorded on the questionnaires is a one-page document consisting of ten points made by a CAFN3 editor. The first three are quoted here (see also Appendix B, #35):

Page 3—Q.6a. The answer to this is usually no. I think people take it to mean 'Have you used a specific method of contraception.' In other words the majority do not include abstinence when answering this question.

Page 5—Q.8a–e. Some answer yes when merely talking of traditional abstinence, others do not.

Page 6—Q.8a–e. Many of the people who say they are pleased merely mean that they accept. In other words they are not pleased in any positive sense.

These, then, are the principal categories of data from which the theory presented in this study was generated. Illustrative examples are cited throughout the text.

Appendix B
Description of Background Documents, with Samples

The *Changing African Family–Nigeria 1973* background documents are available in eleven bound volumes housed in the departmental library, Department of Demography, Research School of Social Sciences, Australian National University, Canberra. The volume titles are as shown below; their contents are grouped and the groups numbered continuously (1–52) throughout the eleven volumes.

Volume I. Misc. Survey Documents: Projects 1, 2, and 3

1. Interviewers' and supervisors' "Block Reports" (*N* = 85). These are reports on survey blocks in Ibadan, prepared for the project directors of CAFN1 after the first ten days in the field. Reports range from two sentences to several paragraphs, averaging one to two paragraphs. [Two examples appear in Appendix A.] A one-page introduction, written by project directors, precedes these reports. The complete introduction:

> The interviewers' block reports which follow represent a very early stage of the survey. After ten days in the field the interviewers were asked to write reports upon progress in their blocks. This was to enable problem areas to be identified and reluctant respondents to be followed up. After this, each interviewer had to go out at least once with a supervisor who established that the area had been fully covered and that those interviewed had fully understood the

questions, especially those relating to contraception. Some of these supervisors' reports are also included in this volume.

It should, therefore, be understood that these reports describe the situation only as it was during the first two weeks of interviewing, and that their very purpose was to point out loose ends and difficulties which needed to be resolved. They are made available in order to pinpoint some of the difficulties in conducting a survey in a vast and largely traditional African town. The final state of the surveying within blocks after a minimum of two supervisory visits per block was very different from that described here. However, it is only through a full appreciation of such problems as are recounted here that those in charge of such surveys can learn just how much supervision and constant contact with the field is necessary, even with the most willing and able teams of interviewers.

Two sample interviewers' reports [examples of supervisors' reports appear in Appendix A]:

Block No. 57
Interviewer: Oyelandun Ayeni
This block lies on the right hand side while going towards Adeoyo hospital on Adeoyo Road, it is 100 yards from the Islamic School and about 8 yards from the main road. I started interviewing from the fourth house to the water pipe, as described in the map.

I interviewed twenty-five women there, since most of them were elderly women, and some were away to the farm and the people didn't know when they would be back. The 25 questionnaires I filled in there were all part 'A', since none of them have ever used contraceptives.

Block No. 65
Interviewer: Olufunmiloke Olnade
This block is on the east side of Ibadan in the Old-Age area. After passing the Aremo-Agugu junction you count four power posts, and by the fifth post on the left you see a footpath road near a big tree, where there is a carpenter—if you go straight in that is the place.

The women were a little difficult because they would say they had heard enough about family planning. I did my best to explain things to them and at last they answered me.

2. A sample of answers to unstructured Question 14, CAFN1, Part B. [This question and two sample answers appear in Chapter 5; see also #40 below.]

3. Sample mappings of the blocks drawn in freehand by supervisors for both CAFN1 and CAFN2.

4. A ten-page, single-spaced "Interviewer's Manual" for CAFN1. Excerpts from the section titled "The Precodes":

> This questionnaire is largely pre-coded. That means that for many of the questions the possible answers are listed with a number beside them and all you have to do is to fill in the number from beside the answer the woman gave in the box to the right. . . .
> This system of using boxes with numbers in allows the answers to be transferred straight to the computer. . . .
> If ever you are not sure which is the coded answer which is closest to the answer given by the woman, or if you think that the answer she gave is not listed at all, then simply WRITE IN the answer given and then ask later in the office what the code should be. We cannot anticipate all possible answers and there are certain to be some cases where there is no code provided on the printed form (although those which come up frequently will be added later).

5. A one-sheet memo with directives to editors of CAFN3 questionnaires. Titled "Final Editing of Project 3," this document encouraged editors to make sure the respondent was eligible and to check against inconsistencies in responses, especially when both husband and wife were interviewed. The first four paragraphs:

> This project is a study of women over 40 years of age who have chosen to have a small family, that is of 5 children or under. One of our main concerns will be therefore to make sure whether or not all the respondents are eligible.
> The following are examples of women who have under 5 children but who are *not* eligible.
> 1. A woman has 2 children but this is because she is not fully fertile, and in fact she very much regrets the fact that she was not able to have a large family.
> 2. A woman has 3 children who die very young, and she has 3 more children to replace them. Although she wanted to have 3 children, and this is what she has, a fact which would seem to make her eligible, she has in fact had 6 live births and is *not* therefore eligible.

6. Records of this final editing work by editors.

7. Directions from Field Director Helen Ware to interviewers for marking precoded, short-answer (semistructured) questions in CAFN3. The final paragraph:

> When coding open-ended questions, use your intelligence and imagination to decide what the person is actually saying, and the code number this fits most closely to. You must *not* code what you think the answer *should* be, in other words you must not let your own opinions influence the coding. It is the respondent's attitude we are interested in and this may be very different from your own. In cases where a certain answer is very common, for which there is no code, it may be possible to create a new code, so you must consult me to discuss this.

8. Directions for sampling in CAFN2. A representative paragraph:

> The basic unit or cluster is the dwelling (house, hut, compound) and every effort is to be made to secure a completed interview with every eligible person in the house. Where the house is entirely Yoruba, you will normally have to interview about half the people living there (the other half will be children 0–16 years of age).

9. An unsolicited 1,200-word essay, written voluntarily by interviewer F.A.O. Adelugba, titled "The Changing African Family Structure—An International Research Project: An Interviewers' Opinion."

Volume II. Project 1 Survey Papers

10. To facilitate hiring fieldworkers, an 8,000- to 10,000-word official description of the Changing African Family project and a cover letter by Field Director Helen Ware to professors in Yorubaland, informing them about the research and requesting them to "bring the enclosed project outline to the attention of your staff and postgraduate students and of anyone else who you feel might be interested."

11. A sample letter of introduction and a sample billfold-size identification card [see Chapter 4] to be carried by interviewers in the field.

12. An early interview schedule for CAFN1 with additional code categories for precoded, short-answer (semistructured) questions written in by hand, showing the process of how the precodes developed.

13. For CAFN1, designated codes for Questions 14–17, 23, 26d, 27f, and 29b–d.

14. For CAFN1, a three-page "Notice to All Interviewers," signed by Field Supervisor Mrs. Shoyinka. The first paragraph:

> Since the survey began we have realised that many interviewers are making the same kind of mistakes in filling in the questionnaires and in coding. Please read the following points VERY CAREFULLY and make sure that in future you do not make the same mistakes.

15. Various supervisory and explanatory memos. Excerpts from supervisory memo written by Pat Caldwell at the end of CAFN1 fieldwork:

> ALL INTERVIEWERS PLEASE NOTE
> You have done a good job with the interviews but there will be some time lag now between this research project and the second project.
> We have to get these questionnaires ready for the computer. That means all office coding must be corrected very quickly and accurately.
> Everyone has to try and learn editing unless they have been given a specific job which keeps them working steadily. Only girls who learn editing can be given continuous employment. . . .
> Editors must record how many interviews they have done, list the errors discovered and what they did about correcting them (this is no criticism of the original interview—everyone makes mistakes). They must also record who did the original interview, her interviewer's number, the block number, who did the first checking and second checking.
> If Mrs. Shoyinka or Dr. Ware has signed it we are satisfied that the computer will not discard it.

And an explanatory memo:

> QUESTION 13
> Some respondents say they are using four codeine tablets together with whisky to wash everything away after they have had sex.
> Will you please separate them from the pill and code as: (xxi) Other.
> All other methods such as long term injection are also entered as (xxi) Other (with written description underneath).

16. A five-page "Editor's Manual" for CAFN1. The first two paragraphs:

> Interviews are people. This means that the whole questionnaire should present a picture of a single personality. When read-

ing through you should always keep in mind the woman's age, education, occupation and number of children.

Page 5—This is still causing much trouble. Q.7 related to what the woman thinks should happen—it should have been answered by everyone including 15 year old school girls. If the girl said she didn't know—refused to have an opinion then code 9 in box 36 and zeros in boxes 37–39.

17. A weekly report form to be filled in by each interviewer in CAFN1. This form required coded information regarding the status of each block for which the interviewer had been responsible during the previous week. Code categories:

   1. Not yet started
   2. Houses listed only
   3. Interviewing just begun
   4. Interviewing ½ completed
   5. Interviewing ¾ completed
   6. Interviewing finished except for 1 woman
   7. Block completed
   8. No eligible women in block

18. A block report form to be filled in by each interviewer and supervisor in CAFN1. [Data from this form resulted in the Block Reports, described in #1, above.]

19. An "Interviewer's Evaluation Sheet" to be completed by the supervisor about the interviewer in CAFN1.

20. An "Editor's Sheet," a sample form designed for CAFN1 editors. It asks for information on the "interviewer who had the block," "most common mistake," the "real problems in coding," and the "general standard of the interviewer."

21. Sample form for delineating the "Interviewer's Monthly Returns."

22. "A Revised List of Additional Codes" for particular questions.

23. "Editing of Project 2," a three-page, single-spaced document giving detailed directions for editing CAFN2. The first paragraph:

   Editing these questionnaires poses some special problems. Since the interviewers are no longer here it is not possible to check any discrepancies with them. Problems that arise have therefore to be sorted out either by using information given in a different part of the questionnaire, or by general discussion to decide the most likely answer.

24. A three-page table giving information about the survey sample centers for CAFN2. Among the data included are 1963 census population statistics for each center.

25. CAFN2 directions and information form for sampling and mapping in Ibadan. Examples:

> Block No. B1—Corner of Oyo Road and Akintola Road opposite Agip Petrol Station.
> Block No. B4—On the north side of Idikan Street immediately west of the Baptist School.
> Block No. B12—On U.I. campus immediately behind the Zoo.

26. "Check list for supervising Project 2 Sites." This list of ten directives for CAFN2 supervisors includes reminders to check maps and make sure houses are properly indicated thereon.

27. Checklist on which CAFN2 fieldworkers are to provide information about the interview centers. This document asks the number of hospitals, doctors, post offices, banks, daily markets; the nearest place to buy condoms or the pill, to have an IUD inserted, or to have an abortion; the number and proximity of schools. It also requires the interviewer to describe in three-line answers to each question the situation with regard to electricity supply, road access, newspapers, cinemas, sewerage facilities, and access to radios. Fieldworkers' responses appear in a document titled "Information Sheets on Individual Centres."

28. A CAFN2 report form for center supervisors to submit to the field director.

29. A CAFN2 two-page form, "Summary Center Report Sheet."

30. A CAFN2 one-page form, "Account of Finished Questionnaires."

31. A CAFN2 one-page form to be used by center editors, requiring them to list "most common mistakes" and to comment on, among other things, the "quality of questionnaire" and the "amount of writing in."

32. A preliminary CAFN3 interview schedule, showing precoded, short-answer question development with new codes written in by hand.

33. The CAFN3 "Interviewer's Manual," explaining who should be interviewed and how. Eight single-spaced pages give detailed directions on selecting a response for each precoded, short-answer question. The three-paragraph section titled "How to Interview":

> Ideally if both husband and wife are eligible (i.e. to be interviewed) they should both be interviewed at the same time but in different rooms. This is why interviewers of alternate sexes have been given adjoining maps so that a girl can go and call on the nearest male interviewer to interview the husband on her map and a man can call on the nearest female interviewer (or on an editor from the office) to interview the wife. However it may not always prove possible to interview the husband and the wife at the same time, and interviewers must use their discretion as to whether to interview the wife when she is available and then to see the husband later.
>
> Where only the woman needs to be interviewed then the interview can be carried out straight away if the woman is willing. There is nothing against male interviewers interviewing women *if* they are certain that the women will not prefer to be interviewed by other women.
>
> Any interviewer who finds a man or woman who, although eligible, refuses to be interviewed must report this fact to the office immediately.

34. A six-page, single-spaced direction sheet for CAFN3, "Final Editing of Project 3."

35. One sheet of ten specific questions or comments by Mrs. Shoyinka after editing CAFN3. [The first three of these appear in Appendix A.] Two examples:

> *Page 11—Q.16.* It is easy to get a wrong impression of the respondent from the answers given in this question. The average traditional Yoruba might very well agree that a small family is less expensive, but this will not prevent him from going ahead and having a large family.
>
> *Page 19—Q.28a.* Difficulty in having a large family is often taken to mean financial and otherwise instead of health. However one can usually obtain an idea of the woman's fertility from the rest of the questionnaire.

36. A six-page document for CAFN3, "Provisional codes for open-ended questions on Project 3."

37. A subsequent document for CAFN3, a sheet of eighteen "New Codes for Boxes 7–10, Page 1, Project 3." For example, new code 8001 was to indicate "Husband not interviewed because dead (but he was monogamous when alive)." New code 8002: "Husband not interviewed because dead (but he was polygamous when alive)." New code 8008: "Wife not interviewed because not living in Ibadan."

38. A CAFN3 memo to interviewers. It specified that Page 3, Box 40 (i.e., the "spare code") was meant to be used as a summary of all methods mentioned previously, and it provided meanings for codes 1 through 9.

39. A CAFN3 two-page form, "Daily Report Sheet," for interviewers.

Volume III. CAFN1: Responses to Questions 14–17 By [Respondents] 0001–6623

40. Typed, "language improved" responses to unstructured CAFN1 Part B, Questions 14–17, for all subjects (*N* = 1,050) who answered Part B. [Sample responses to Question 14 also appear in Volume I; see #2 above.] Two of the questions, each followed by sample answers (preceded by the # symbol) from the same two respondents:

> *Question 14.* Can you remember when you first thought that you might some day practise family planning? What kind of thing had happened that made you think these things? Can you tell me just how this came into your mind at just that time?
> (Probe and write down in detail everything that the respondent said went on in her mind and what had happened at that time.)
> #*0001.* When she was in [nursing] training she use the safe period method because in her institution she must not be pregnant or else she will be sent out.
> #*0002.* I started practicing rhythm in 1971. This came into my mind because I was forced by my fiancé at that time.

> *Question 16.* When you made up your mind to use family planning, what were the circumstances that made you come to this decision? Why did you do it? What had happened at that time?
> #*0001.* Because of her training and no girl should be in the family way.
> #*0002.* The circumstances that made me come to this decision was that I do not want to be pregnant at that time. And I did it because my fiancé forced me.

Volume IV. CAFN2: Daily Reports and Selected Responses

41. A thirty-four-page, typed, double-spaced set of eleven "Daily Reports of
Interviewing at Centers." These were prepared by one interviewer at each
of eleven CAFN2 centers during July 1973. Some daily entries say only,
"Interviews continued"; others are several paragraphs long. Each entire
report ranges in length from 2 to 7 pages, with the mode $(N = 5)$ being
3 pages. Excerpts from the Ikere-Ekiti and Orun report:

> *7th July, 1973*
> The three of us, Miss Adedeji, Mr. Edwin and Adelola went round
> the town [Ikere] to locate the clusters.
> *8th July, 1973*
> We started mapping of the clusters.
> *9th July, 1973*
> Mapping and visit to the local school Board and Health office, to
> collect information about number of schools and health workers in
> the town.
> *10th July, 1973*
> Completion of mapping work, numbering of the houses and
> visiting area to locate the selected houses. Adelola went to the
> District Hospital with the supervisor, Mr. Orubuloye, to complete
> the hospital section of the information sheet.
> *11th July, 1973*
> We started interview today and we completed ten question-
> naires. Miss Adenike Adeliloye was sent from Ado to join us, by the
> supervisor. . . .
> *13th July, 1973*
> The supervisor, Mr. I. Orubuloye, joined us at 9 A.M. and worked
> with us until about 3:30 P.M. We interviewed people in block VI
> house A1, block VII house A and we found nobody at home in
> block V house A. We went back to block I where we interviewed
> three people, two women refused interview, despite persuasion by
> the supervisor and we ended the day's work by completing the inter-
> view of respondent 3 in block 2, house A which has been started by
> Adeliloye on Thursday.
> *14th July, 1973*
> We visited many houses but most of the people have gone to the
> farm to take food in preparation for the week-end.
> *15th July, 1973*
> The people were not available for interview until after the

morning service. Attempts to track some down after the service
failed. . . .

17th July, 1973

We went round the houses where the are eligible people who
have not been interviewed and to complete those partly done. The
supervisor visited us today and passed her instructions to us.

18th July, 1973

We conducted some interviews and went round the houses to
find out the religion of the people. Some of the people have gone to
their farms, but those who were in helped us. We made necessary
corrections on the questionnaires and completed the information
sheets.

19th July, 1973—Orun

Four of us, Miss F. Adedeji, Mr. Orubuloye, Edwin and Adelola
went to Orun, drew the map of the village, numbered the houses
and visited the selected houses.

20th July, 1973

Mr. J. Adedara joined us and we started interviews. Most of the
selected houses we visited were empty in the morning because the
people have gone to the farm. Some of the people we interviewed
today came back from the farm in the afternoon.

21st July, 1973

Today is the market day and most of the women went to the
market and the men did not return from the farm until very late. . . .

26th July, 1973

We worked until about 2 p.m. when there was heavy rain.

27th July, 1973

It was not possible to get the people interviewed because they
came late from the farm and we worked until dawn.

28th July, 1973

Completion of the information sheets and necessary corrections
of the questionnaires were done.

42. "Selected Responses to Individual Questions, Project 2," typed, "language improved." These are representative samples of verbatim answers to the open-ended, short-answer questions in CAFN2. Sample answers to Q.31a, asking how a man with two wives, twelve children, and little money "got into this situation" [see Chapter 5 for the question and Chapter 6 for additional responses]:

#2159. He caused the situation himself. He should not have up to twelve children when he knows he cannot provide for them.

#2051. Greediness in the acquisition of children and lack of planning.

#2052. They are in the situation because the family cannot cut its coat according to its size.

#2053. The man couldn't control his sexual urge and is ignorant of contraception and abortion.

#2182. The man must have been thinking that he would be able to train the few who would train others and thereby have a large family with many of them able to help educate them in their society. But his failure must have been due to his miscalculation as far as the rapidity with which he had given birth.

#2692. This is due to his greed in having two wives who would like to have as many children as possible.

And another example question, followed by all listed (*N* = 5) responses:

Q.(33). Think of all the things that might happen to you if you were very lucky. What would be the best thing that could possibly happen to you?

#2159. I want plenty of money, good health.

#2160. I would like to win a lottery and invest the money in lots of farming projects.

#2080. I want to have a baby as soon as possible.

#2169. I want to win a big amount that I can use to establish myself.

#2281. Being a very rich man.

Volume V. CAFN2: Responses to Questions 33–36c

43. Photocopies of page 12 of every tenth CAFN2 interview schedule, showing open-ended, short-answer questions 33 through 36c with responses written in.

Volume VI. CAFN2: Responses to Questions 45b–47b

44. Photocopies of page 15 of every tenth CAFN2 interview schedule, showing open-ended, short-answer questions 45b through 47b with responses written in.

Volume VII. CAFN2: Responses to Question 48a–48e

45. Photocopies of page 16 of every tenth CAFN2 interview schedule, showing open-ended, short-answer questions 48a through 48e, with responses written in.

Volume VIII. CAFN2: Final Notes

46. Photocopies of all completed final pages of the CAFN2 interview schedule. A blank page headed "Final Notes," requested the interviewer to write in his or her summary comments about the interview. A slightly longer than average example:

> The man is a tailor and is 20 years old. He has not married because he has just finished his apprenticeship. He wishes to work and save before he marries. I met him in one of the shops in his house. I visited him twice before I could finish my interview with him. The reason why it was so long was that he was busy with his work and went out to collect materials for his work.
>
> His income is very low since he has just established. He read up to primary six and he is alive to see the conditions of the married people. Therefore, he decided in his mind to marry one wife and have about seven children. He determines to do family planning when he marries. He does not support the idea of having many wives and children. He feels that one must not live beyond one's means. He added that one must educate one's children in order to prevent poverty.

A second, still longer, example:

> The man is a barber and he said he has small farm where he produces food crops. He has one wife and he said that he has no hope of marrying the second one. He emphasized that having the second wife would not only be a burden on him, but also a burden for the first wife. He welcomed me to his place of living. A sitting room and a sleeping room.
>
> I visited the man four times and during the last two I collected the answers from him. The reason why I could not collect the information at once was that he always comes late from his place of work everyday. He spends few hours with his family. He hesitated to answer some questions, but he was persuaded to give few answers. The reason is that he is a semi-literate man. He wishes his

children to be six, at present he has five. The income of his wife and that of [himself] is poor. They do not want to have many children they would be unable to cater for. The family wishes to do family planning. He told me that if they are fortunate to become rich in the future, they would have at least two more to make eight. To lessen his problem, he sent two of his children to his mother to help her and he does not want another child who does not belong to him. He said that he and his wife are very fond of themselves [one another]. He added that he is not in support of people who would like to have many children and would not be able to cater for them. He added that if one is so rich and sees that one's income can be sufficient for three wives, one could try to have them. He said that they get great advantages from the Methodist and state hospitals which are in their town. He added that if he had been in the rural areas where there is no medical facilities, he would have stopped at the fourth child. From my own point of view, though a semiliterate, he reaches the value of having a few children.

Volume IX.   CAFN3:   Commentary on Respondents in Project 3

47. A thousand-word "Introduction" to the "Commentary on Respondents" of [#48 below]. Excerpts from the document:

The respondents eligible to be interviewed in the Achieved Small Family Study were all Yoruba women, resident in Ibadan, who were aged forty or above and had had five or fewer children (live-births) by choice. The husbands were also eligible for interview where the wives were still in their first marriages. Under African conditions it is not a simple matter to establish either age or parity, especially when the respondents are women approaching the menopause who have had but little education, need to be concerned with dates of birth, or desire to recall children long dead. However, techniques have been devised to secure the most accurate information possible on these counts, and, with patience, it is possible to establish whether the required criteria have been satisfied. . . .

The comments presented here are provided for those using the data sets associated with Project 3 . . . to provide a clear picture of the difficulties associated with determining eligibility, and the different types of eligibility involved. They should be read with this purpose in mind and with an understanding that statistics represent complex people not simple abstractions.

To facilitate identification of respondents within these different categories, each respondent is coded with one of the following numbers.

(1) Planned a small family [fewer than five children] early in marriage, and used contraception (including rhythm and withdrawal) to achieve this aim.

(2) Planned a small family early in marriage but only used prolonged abstinence to achieve this aim.

(3) Cases in which the decision to have a small family only came after several children had been born, where planning consisted more in determining 'this is enough' than in forward planning from the start. Also cases where element of planning much weaker than in (1) or (2).

(4) Eligible—wish to have five or fewer children, but currently below that limit and either pregnant or wish to have one more child.

(5) Women who decided not to remmarry when widowed *because* they did not wish to have any more children.

(6) Cases where the respondents are inherently pronatalist, but where owing to circumstances (such as the neglect of the husband, their own ill-health, etc.) they chose to limit the size of their families. The implication is that they were forced into having small families, but that the small family was achieved by voluntary fertility restriction.

(7) Borderline cases where it is difficult to distinguish between choice of the small family and passive acceptance of it, often associated with a degree of infertility or infant mortality. Includes cases such as that in which the respondent claims only to have wanted four children but in fact only had two due to infertility.

[There is no (8) in this document.]

(9) The most borderline cases of all.

48. "Commentary on Respondents in Project 3." Fieldworkers' comments, requested in the questionnaire, regarding the CAFN3 eligibility and the assigned respondent eligibility code [see #47 above] for each female subject. Examples (the number in parentheses following each entry is the eligibility code):

#0008. Definitely eligible—did not want to have more than 5 children. (2)

#0047. Abstinence—no evidence it was a choice. Said no difficulty in conceiving. Long spacing. (3)

#*0048.* One child only due to very painful childbirth. Used abortion and condoms. (1)

#*0151.* Not eligible—when she wanted a fourth child she was no longer able to conceive. Would have liked as many children as God gave her. (9)

#*0175.* Eligible—Woman had 5 children between 1934–1948. All 4 but the last one died in 1949 or 1950. She was told by a herbalist that the other wives had poisoned her children and she decided to divorce her husband and be happy with the one child left. She is eligible in as far as she didn't go to another man. (2)

#*0186.* Eligible—She had 5 births out of which one died. She used abstinence and rhythm. Believes that one is helping the nation in having a small number of children. (1)

#*0193.* Deliberately stopped after 5th birth so as to educate them. (1)

#*0251.* The woman has only 1 child and wants a bigger family (although only 5). Almost certainly subfertile. Had her 1 child in 1964, said to be 40 and married between 25–30. (7)

#*0489.* Query—didn't have few children by choice—says it is God's work. But she seems quite happy with the number she has. (6)

#*0491.* I.U.D. and self-induced abortion. Has 5 children. (1)

#*0492.* Only used up to 2 years abstinence. Says that what she did was nice since husband was dead, and to remarry was intolerable to her. (5)

#*0495.* Is obviously in favour of having a small family, and explains carefully how she spaced her family. Does not however specifically say that she stopped at the 5th. (3)

49. "Selected Responses to Individual Questions in the Achieved Small Family, Project 3." These are sample verbatim responses (N = 1 to N = 24) to short-answer CAFN3 questions. One question with responses (H = husband; W = wife):

Q.*20(iii).* Would you regard it as a tragedy if you were not succeeded by descendants? (IF YES) Why? What would be the worst things about having no descendants?

#*0003.* (W) It is ill luck for anybody who has no descendants because her property will pass to other people after her death.

#*0005.* (W) No one to bury one after death.

#*0007.* (W) It will be very bad if one has no descendants for a Yoruba says those people who have no children are natural servants or followers.

#0010. (H) By having no descendant it is regarded as a great tragedy as regard to Yoruba tradition.

#0014. (W) In Yoruba it is a great prestige to be succeeded by children.

#0016. (W) She said that it will be a tragedy if she has no son because there will be nobody to be the pillar of the house after death.

#0020. (H) It is too bad not having any children because all your goods will be given to relatives who have been saying bad things about you.

#0022. (W) It is a bad thing for not having children in both sex, not to talk of having none, because no one is going to bury the woman.

#0027. (W) It means that there is nobody to look after him or her after the old age and no one to share one's property, which is bad.

#0029. (H) Some one having no descendant is aimless in this world.

#0033. (W) If one does not have descendants one may not have proper burial and may easily be forgotten.

#0034. (W) After her death there would be no one to attend to her funeral.

#0036. (W) There must be descendants who will give proper funeral for the parents.

#0039. (W) It is not a good thing to leave this world without descendants because if one has none, the person may not be respectedly buried.

50. "Comments from Final Page of Questionnaires, Project 3." A full empty page was attached to the back of each CAFN3 questionnaire [as with CAFN2; see #46, above] with the directive to the interviewer to write comments after the interview. This document includes complete verbatim comments for all (*N* = 509) CAFN3 respondents. Comments range from one sentence to four paragraphs, averaging one five-line (typed) paragraph. Four examples:

#0191. This man appears to be friendly when I first start the interview but there were some questions which he didn't want to answer until he was petted a lot.

#0192. The woman said she is not pleased about this number of children but at the other hand she is happy that her two children are taking care of her.

#0197. The woman is 55 years old her age is too low compare

with the age of her husband she married her husband when she was 26 and her husband was 48 by then third wife. She is not living with her husband but he comes to her at times. She has four children by choice but the last one died. She is still satisfy with the three that they remain. None of her children has married.

#0508. I first came across this woman yesterday but I did not interview her because I thought she was not eligible as she told me that her husband has four wives and she is the 2nd wife and that she has four children on the order of her husband. She said that the husband said that each of the wives will have only four children each. She said that she wanted to have more but her husband refused. She said she should have divorced the husband but she could not do so because of her four children.

I interview her today because of the advice from Dr. Ware. I could observe that the woman is not satisfied with her condition i.e. she was not pleased to have only four children but her hands are tied because she is a full housewife without any reasonable income. I also had a chat with the husband who told me he has four wives out of ignorance and now that he has realised that his income cannot cope with more than very few children he has come to the conclusion of total abstention as he needs no more children as he could not train them. I could see that the man has eighteen children and their education is just primary six.

Volume X. CAFN3: Responses to Question 23

51. All responses (N = 509) to open-ended, short-answer CAFN3 Question 23. The question, with examples of answers:

Q.23. We have asked you a lot of questions about your feelings about having planned a fairly small family. Perhaps we have not asked the right questions. Tell us in your own words what you feel about what you have done, and what are the good things about it and what are the bad things.

#0001. In fact with the small number of children, we (my husband and myself) were able to train them and God himself gives them a very bright brain so they were able to become an important persons in the city today. I thank God for I do not regret on this limitation of children. Only one of them died in a motor accident in 1970. And in fact the rest don't allow me to regret or become sad since then.

#0004. In fact I do not pray for only one child but as God would have it, I had one and I could not change this. I thank Him in giving me a dutiful daughter who gives me money and all things that I need.

#0005. I do not see any bad thing in it for they do care for me.

#0006. Having only one son does not make me happy at all, but I thank God as half bread is better than none. I could have had two children but I had one miscarriage and since then I did not get pregnant again.

#0011. We planned for a small family in order to cater for them as far as their education is concerned before their father retired from work. We are happy now that we are heading to our aim.

#0119. We first thought of having just two children but on the long run we decided to have two more.

#0510. Throughout my life time I abstained up to three years. I had four children—two boys and two girls. Now there are three remaining. They were all given chance to go to school, but the two girls stopped in primary six. The senior one who is a boy read up to school certificate class.

Volume XI. CAFN3: Responses to Questions 8g–47a

52. Selected samples of verbatim responses (N = 1 to N = 50) to short-answer questions in CAFN3. Examples of questions and their answers:

Q.8g. What kinds of things do relatives say about the size of your family and the fact that you limited it?

#0001. Some even pray that theirs should be like me. For all my children were well educated.

#0002. I have two live births but the two children had died. They pray to God for me so that I may have issue in my life.

#0007. They usually say that I should have more especially my husband's relatives.

#0011. They told me that the size of my family is too small. And since there is no financial problem that I should continue having children up to eight.

#0013. Most of my relatives even advised me to limit my family since my husband had five wives. So they said that the size of my family is good as it is now.

#0451. Our parents being that they are old do not support the idea of a planned family but our younger brothers and sisters like the size of our family.

#0108. I limited the number of children because I used to find child birth very painful. My relatives do not say much about the size of my children since I have a reason.

Q.9a(i) Are there any disadvantages now in having a family of your size?

#0006. If I have had more children [than one son], there will be someone to look after me as my son is always away from home on tour, if even I have a girl she will take care of me better but I still thank God for the only one I have for he is trying his best to satisfy me.

Q.10b(ii). Can you see any advantages in the future in having a family of your size? If yes, what?

#0013. The advantages in the future in having a family of this size are that my children will be happy since they will be educated like boys of their age and as such they will be able to earn their living and support their family too.

#0005. My children will be able to educate their children to any level so far they themselves were educated.

Q.13b. Amongst the people you live with, does the size of your family affect their regard for you and how important they think you are? In other words, is your prestige affected in the eyes of your relatives? What about the other people who live in the area you live in? How is your prestige affected?

#0001. They do give a very high prestige because of the successful children I have.

#0002. My mates are now given more prestige than myself, for their children have grown up and become important persons unlike me who has no child left.

#0004. My daughter is now in her husband's house. She is a trader. She has a big shop, so with her position in our house, people look at me very high.

#0013. My prestige was affected due to the ways I control my children and because I have the highest number of educated children among my husband's wives.

#0463. My prestige is affected during annual festivals or family gathering when I have few children around me.

Q.46a. Did you feel that you were breaking with tradition in having a small family?

#0012. As things are changing everyday it is good to move with time so I think I was breaking with tradition in having a small family.

Notes

Chapter 1. Introduction

1. Between 1972 and 1975 demographers undertook parallel studies in eleven African countries representing its various regions: in North Africa, Tunisia and Sudan; in Francophone West Africa, Senegal, Upper Volta, and Togo; in Anglophone West Africa, Ghana and Nigeria; in Middle Africa, Cameroon, the Congo, and Zaire; and in East Africa, Kenya and Uganda.

2. For a complementary description of the CAFN research, see Okediji et al., 1976.

3. It should be noted that the figures for Nigeria are estimated from a 1963 national census, which yielded data with various inconsistencies and returned a population figure of 55.7 million, now thought to have been inflated. The latest census conducted in Nigeria was in 1973, but the results were subsequently canceled because the obtained population of 79.8 million was thought to have been grossly inflated. Thus, data from the 1963 census remain officially the most current, and all *official* population estimates and projections are based on them (World Fertility Survey, 1984: 5).

4. Because official census data are old and unreliable (see note 3), I rely on data from CAFN itself for a description of Yorubaland in the 1970s. Data presented in this section are taken from CAFN2, which surveyed 1,497 Yoruba males and 1,499 Yoruba females throughout Western and Lagos states in Nigeria.

5. The Caldwells defined white-collar occupations as all professional, administrative, clerical, and other occupations (such as military and police officers or government messengers) that were nonmanual and necessitated literacy (Caldwell, 1977a: 14).

6. Yorubas belong to one of the few ethnic groups in tropical Africa where the women do not do most of the farming (Caldwell, 1976a: 198).

7. For descriptions of Yoruba markets, see Clapperton (1829: 12); and Fadipe (1970: 159–63).

8. In 1973, Western education correlated negatively with age. Of those aged 50 and older, 80 percent had no Western schooling. The proportion was

143

70 percent for those in their 40s; 56 percent for those in their 30s; 30 percent for those in their 20s. Among respondents under age 20, the figure was only 14 percent.

Fosterage, described in Chapters 6 and 7, helped in children's education. In the early 1970s about two-thirds of urban white-collar homes housed others' children, typically to permit them to go to school. Forty percent of village farm families had children living elsewhere, three-quarters of those for reasons of education (Caldwell, 1976a: 219–20).

9. Data presented on CAFN2 survey locations were compiled in the field by the project's interviewers and supervisors.

10. Typical factories in Yorubaland included a brewery and a weaving center in Abeokuta; textile and saw mills, a printing press, a cement block factory, and a tire-retreading center in Ondo.

11. The estimated populations of Ibadan and Lagos in 1975 were 847,000 and 1,061,000, respectively ("Nigeria," 1991: 1948).

12. The Yoruba word for compound translates literally as "a flock of houses" (Fadipe, 1970: 97). The typical "flock" was made up of small adjoining apartments used for sleeping and storing personal possessions. The quadrangle they enclosed was a common open space in which poultry, sheep, or goats might roam. A roofed verandah, about eight feet wide, ran round the inner walls of the compound and opened onto the quadrangle. Unlike the rooms behind it, the verandah was not partitioned. Here adults and children ate, drank, and wandered freely.

Usually the eldest male member headed the compound, establishing order and allocating communal land. Generally, each husband had his own room, as did each wife, whether a man was monogamously or polygynously married. On the verandah adjacent to her room, each wife maintained her own kitchen. Polygynous wives customarily observed an "order of seniority to which rights and duties attach[ed]," depending on the length of time they had lived in the compound (Fadipe, 1970: 114). Young children slept with their mothers. Older children, particularly males, often occupied a separate room or slept on the verandah (Fadipe, 1970: 97–103; see also Eades, 1980: 45–49).

13. At any given time, probably about one-half of Yorubas reside in polygynous unions in which the man has two to eight (sometimes more) wives. Over a lifetime the potential for being polygynously married increases (Caldwell and Caldwell, 1987: 420; see also Caldwell, 1976a and 1977a).

Chapter 2. Historical Prelude

1. Among those with specialized craft occupations were general carpenters, mask and calabash carvers, leather workers, potters, drummers and

bards, herbalists, and the surgeons who did facial and body scarring (Bascom, 1969: 98–112; Fadipe, 1970: 153). Among the women were soap and indigo dye makers and basket and textile weavers. Some women dressed hair or did tatooing; others produced camwood dye for body cosmetics. Women also specialized in food preparation: one might fix yams or beans in a particular way, for example, while another would be known for preparing them differently (Fadipe, 1970: 151–52).

2. Samir Amin (1976: 200) has argued that this "ruin of the crafts" is characteristic of a society's transition to peripheral capitalism. "The onslaught from without, by means of trade, carried out by the capitalist mode of production upon the precapitalist formations, causes certain crucial retrogressions to take place, such as the ruin of the crafts without their being replaced by local industrial production."

3. Before Europeans introduced guns, traditional hunters hunted rats, squirrels, monkeys, porcupine, warthog, water-buck, and birds with wooden clubs or bows and iron-tipped arrows. They set iron traps, using jungle creepers and climbers as ropes; they also dug pits to trap big game and asphyxiated smaller animals in their burrows. "The rare chase was made up of the really wild animals such as buffaloes, lions, leopards, hyenas, wild dogs, and elephants" (Ojo, 1966: 33).

4. Direct taxation was met with major protests in Abeokuta. In response, "a thousand troops were brought in and five hundred insurgents killed" (Isichei, 1983: 398).

5. In 1986 an estimated 12 percent of the labor force was unemployed. In 1988, the Nigerian government reported an inflation rate of 25 percent; other estimates suggested that it might be as high as 40 percent ("Nigeria," 1991: 1946).

6. A crossed-out clause in Beecroft's appointment document stated that the government had "no intention to seek to gain possession, either by purchase or otherwise, of any portion of the African Continent in those parts" (Isichei, 1983: 362).

7. When in 1916 a group of Yorubas burned government buildings in protest, "the Government sternly repressed the revolt, hanging about fourteen of its ringleaders" (Buell, 1928: 708).

8. Lines from a timely prayer to Sango, God of Thunder, are telling: "Sango, if you don't bless me I'll go and turn Christian. But Sango, if you do bless me, Elephant-with-eyes-as-large-as-water-drums, . . . I say I won't turn Christian" (quoted in Barber, 1981: 737).

Chapter 3. The Yoruba Fieldworkers

1. In order to minimize interviewer effects, most respondents were interviewed by fieldworkers of the same sex. Hence CAFN1 fieldworkers were almost all females; CAFN2 fieldworkers were males and females; and males questioned the 71 husbands interviewed in CAFN3.

2. Data from such forms resulted in CAFN1 Block Reports (Appendix B, #1) and CAFN2 Daily Reports (Appendix B, #41).

3. If one response of interviwers to the supervision network was to provide performance explanations to superiors, another was to form teams or alliances of their own in the field. A daily report from Odogbolu and Isiwo, for example, relates that when "members of the [interviewer] group met for the first time, formal introductions were made and the group was born." After the first day's work, the team "returned to Itanna rest-house, the Base from which Odogbolu group would operate." Thereupon, after "views were exchanged by members of the group," the emergent team "ended the day with [a] game of What" (CAFN2-r: p. 1). Such teamwork—the field equivalent of the nightly gatherings at headquarters—boosted morale, helped to legitimate the project for the subordinates themselves, and provided for more efficient fieldwork.

4. See Map 2 in Chapter 4.

Chapter 4. Gaining Entrance

1. Researchers "offered respondents their traditional language, and we invariably greeted them first in that language. As a result, although we were assured by many other researchers and officials that a very substantial proportion of the respondents in Ibadan would opt to be interviewed wholly in English (as has been the case in a good deal of research there) in fact less than 6 percent did so" (Okediji et al, 1976: 134).

2. Some signs of Westernization, such as clothing, could make gaining entry more difficult, however. As one male interviewer reported, "The old man seemed very critical of anybody in shirt and trousers. I have to persuade him for about an hour before he volunteered to respond to the questions posed" (CAFN2-fn: 1602).

3. This may have resulted in part from the statement in introduction to the CAFN1 questionnaire that "this is an important piece of research which will be useful for social planning."

4. But interviewers, particularly those who advanced to become supervisors, necessarily challenged this. Indeed, their continued employment required doing so: "Interviewers who proved unable to take part in discussing [private topics such as birth control usage] freely with individuals from all

social classes were not employed beyond the pilot stage" (Caldwell and Ware, 1977: 489).

5. Interviewers were strongly motivated to obtain answers to CAFN1's Part B: on a point system that helped in rating their performance, they received two points for completing a Part B, but only one for a Part A.

Chapter 5. The Lessons Inherent in the Projects

1. According to the bound marginals (see Appendix A), of the total CAFN2 sample, 93.2 percent (91.6 percent of men and 94.7 percent of women) said "no good thing"; another 1.2 percent said they didn't know; 0.9 percent said economic advantage; and 4.1 said freedom from responsibilities (0.6 percent gave other, miscellaneous responses).

2. Of those who were currently married in the CAFN2 sample ($N = 2,232$), less than half of 1 percent said they disliked their spouses; 9 percent said they respected but did not have a close relationship with their partners; 13 percent said they were "fairly fond" and 53 percent "very fond" of the spouse; 24 percent said they were "very much in love."

3. Of those who were currently married in the CAFN2 sample ($N = 2,232$), 35 percent slept in the same room with the spouse; 52 percent slept in the same house or compound but not the same room; 5 percent slept in the same compound but not in the same building; 8 percent lived even farther apart but did not define themselves as separated.

Forty-eight percent neither ate, sat at parties, nor visited friends together; approximately 22 percent said they did so occasionally; 30 percent answered "yes" to these questions.

4. "When we have discussed fosterage in Africa and have included the most common form, that of adopting nieces and nephews, there have invariably been protests that this is not fosterage at all. We have been repeatedly told that this is a foreign distinction and that nephews and nieces have the same rights of accommodation and support as biological offspring, and that a child who felt any emotional deprivation or who protested at being transferred from parents to uncle and aunt would be abnormal or wicked. They are, in effect, still in the same lineage accommodation" (Caldwell and Caldwell, 1987: 419).

5. Eighty-six percent of the respondents (88 percent of males and 85 percent of females) said the money spent was greater than the value of the children's earnings and productive work. Whether the respondents agreed that this situation necessarily made parents financially worse off is not clear.

6. Thirty percent of the sample (36 percent of males and 23 percent of females) said they had never used anything, not even abstinence. Another 59 percent (52 percent of males and 66 percent of females) said they had

used postnatal abstinence only; 9.5 percent had used or were currently using contraceptives, with 4.8 percent of the sample (5.1 percent of males and 4.5 percent of females) currently doing so. The remainder gave no response.

7. "Much effort was also put into identifying all birth control methods and all Yoruba terms, both respectable and less respectable, for every method. Interviewers were trained and tested repeatedly in their use, and in describing methods in detail because frequently practices are employed without being named" (Caldwell and Ware, 1977: 489).

8. Cicourel (1974: 188) has argued this same point with regard to fertility research in Argentina.

9. Fourteen percent (17 percent of males and 12 percent of females) said they would prefer ten children to six; 6 percent said they would prefer more than ten; 70 percent (67 percent of males and 73 percent of females) said they would prefer six or fewer; 10 percent said they didn't know or gave no response.

10. Seventy-six percent of respondents (N = 793) said their husbands definitely knew that they were using a contraceptive method, and 20 percent (N = 203) said their husbands did not know. Seventy-three percent of the women (N = 770) had talked about it with their husbands, while 21 percent (N = 225) had not. In both cases, the remainder refused to answer.

11. Eighteen percent of the sample (N = 540) said they did not want another child, but this figure includes the widowed and separated. Another 10 percent said they were not married. Of the 2,155 remaining, 48 percent (N = 1,044) said they wanted more children but would not be very disappointed if they decided it would be better not to have another child; 39 percent (N = 841) said they wanted more children and would be very disappointed; 8 percent (N = 182) said they didn't know; and 5 percent (N = 88) refused to answer.

12. This was an unstructured, open-ended question, in which the interviewer was directed only to elicit and write in comments, which would be coded later. Interestingly, two responses ("There is no problem," and "They should accept it, it depends on God, there is nothing that they can do") were subsequently coded "resignation" by the principal researchers, a value-laden label carrying negative connotations within the world view of efficacy.

13. A body of demographic literature addresses problems in ascertaining accurate ages for Third World subjects. For one thing, Third World age data are typically characterized by "heaping," usually at digits ending in 0 and 5 and to a lesser extent at 2 and 4. This is due not only to "rounding" but also to the tendency of both respondents and fieldworkers to prefer or to avoid certain digits. Demographers have developed indices (e.g., the Myers's, the Whipple's, and the Mortara's) that approximate the extent of traditional pref-

erence for or avoidance of various digits in the Third World (Caldwell and Ware, 1977: 489; World Fertility Survey 1984: 41).

14. Hence many Yorubas, both CAFN subjects and those enumerated by censuses, could not provide accurate age information (Caldwell and Igun, 1971: 287). A little less than half (49 percent) of CAFN2 respondents felt sure about their age. Another 27 percent were doubtful. In 18 percent of the cases, the interviewer estimated the subject's age; in 6 percent age information was offered by a third person.

Chapter 6. Resisting the Lessons

1. Interviewers could lie too, of course—for example, to gain entrance: "I promised her that something very tangible is coming for her from the Department of Sociology, U.I. [University of Ibadan]" (CAFN2-fn: 1186).

2. It is not possible to tell from the data what proportion of respondents who said "nothing" meant this literally and what proportion used this response as a means of avoiding the calculus required by the question.

3. Just 9.5 percent of CAFN2 respondents said they had ever used contraceptive methods other than abstinence, rhythm, or withdrawal.

4. Schools are, after all, "rows or ranks of pupils in the class, corridors, courtyards; rank attributed to each pupil at the end of each task and each examination; the rank he obtains from week to week, month to month, year to year; an alignment of age groups, one after another; a succession of subjects taught and questions treated, according to an order of increasing difficulty. And, in this ensemble of compulsory alignments, each pupil, according to his age, his performance, his behaviour, occupies sometimes one rank, sometimes another" (Foucault, 1975: 147).

Chapter 7. The CAFN Projects as World-System Demography

1. As was true at the time of the CAFN projects, today's demography is largely funded through United States corporate foundations and government agencies. Despite refusing to fund abortions since the mid-1980s, United States Aid to International Development (USAID) continues to be the largest single funder of fertility research and control in the Third World (Crane and Finkle 1989; Demerath, 1976; Hartmann, 1987; Hodgson, 1988). The United Nations Fund for Population Activities (UNFPA) is the second largest donor of international population assistance (Crane and Finkle, 1989: 23). Because of the official U.S. position on abortion, USAID withdrew funding for UNFPA in 1985, but Japan is expected to fill that gap (Crane and Finkle 1989). While it is too early to be certain, it appears now that Japan is committed to fol-

lowing the modernization–interventionist paradigm initiated and set by the United States.

2. In Caldwell's model, nucleation is the independent variable negatively related to upward intergenerational wealth flow, an intervening variable (Caldwell, 1980: 241–42), and hence positively correlated with a diminished kin-controlled structure demanding high fertility (Caldwell and Caldwell, 1987: 420).

3. Critics have argued that by focusing on Third World fertility, vested and often concealed interests in the First World have diverted attention from issues of wealth and power distribution (Bondestam and Bergstrom, 1980; Chamberlain, 1974; George, 1977; Hartmann, 1987; Hofsten, 1980; Mamdani, 1972; Patterson and Shrestha, 1988). Lars Bondestam (1980: 12) has argued that "the wealthy sensed a menace to the unequal consumption of the world's resources and to a continued exploitation of raw products and cheap labour of the periphery" and therefore reiterated the importance of family planning. Amin too (1976: 358) has postulated that First World fertility rhetoric is motivated by fear: "The world campaign for birth control in the Third World expresses, in fact, the fears of the developed countries faced with the danger of a radical challenge to the international order by the peoples who have been its first victims. . . . If the masses of the Third World could divert . . . resources and exploit them for their own benefit, the conditions under which the capitalist system functions at the center would be upset." Demographer Geoffrey McNicoll (1988) has offered a selection of subtly frightening scenarios of the world's future in light of "North/South" wealth and population disparities.

4. In a 1969 presidential message on population, Richard Nixon called for the United Nations to take a leading role in Third World population control. That same year the UNFPA was established, but it has for the most part followed United States leadership. USAID, "established first," announced its Director R. T. Ravenholt, "is ahead of the U.N., which will follow trails blazed by AID" (quoted in Hartmann, 1987: 106).

5. In 1944 demographer and sociologist Kingsley Davis recognized imperialism as a factor in poverty formation. Sounding much like contemporary world-system theorists, he argued that because of the West's "monopoly over the virgin resources and expanding markets of the entire world," India had become "a satellite nation" (quoted in Hodgson, 1983: 14). Generally, Davis held that prior industrial emergence in the West and subsequent political and economic domination over other regions hampered the latter's industrialization opportunities. Unlike critical social scientists, however, Davis did not consider redistribution of global wealth as an essential component in any solution; a student of Talcott Parsons at Harvard (Mullins, 1973: 45–72), he was very much in the flow of mainstream sociological structure-

functionalism. For Davis and the functionalists, social inequality would always be "an unconsciously evolved device by which societies insure that the most important positions are conscientiously filled by the most qualified persons" (Davis and Moore, 1945: 243). If one were to extend Davis's argument to a global context, it would follow that world leadership is as it should be. Davis's solution to Third World poverty was that First World leaders should intervene to influence worldwide population reduction. Since traditional cultures had already been modified by colonial domination, he argued, "perhaps they can be modified with regard to fertility as well" (quoted in Hodgson, 1983: 16–17).

6. In the orthodox view, high Third World fertility was due to lack of appreciation for or access to modern contraceptives. Accordingly, the movement introduced birth control programs in numerous Third World nations. "Organized family planning programs, at least as a matter of avowed policy, now cover the large majority of the population of the developing world" (Demeny, 1988: 468). Indeed, the impact of the family planning establishment can hardly be overestimated today. Its influence "is well indicated by the now thoroughly muddied distinction between family planning as a term (once a euphemism) for fertility regulation by an individual or couple and family planning as a shorthand for an organized promotional activity and supply system, typically run or overseen by government" (McNicoll, 1988: 13).

7. In "a bold attack on the whole demographic transition concept" (Freedman, 1982: 261), Caldwell argued as early as the 1960s that high fertility in West Africa was reasonable; hence, just making contraceptives available was not an answer. Caldwell blamed demographers' failure to appreciate this on the fact that his colleagues were "often extraordinarily ethnocentric" (Caldwell, 1976a: 245). He later declared that "Western ethnocentricity has bedeviled Third World research and introduced wholly inappropriate attitudes, assumptions and methods" (Caldwell, 1982b: 148). Nevertheless, he gradually assumed a central position within mainstream demography.

8. Demography, like all science, is imbued with the classical enlightenment notion of progress through reason. Progress in the Third World, it is commonly assumed, will emerge only with the diminution of anachronistic "accretions of superstition, misunderstanding, and ignorance" (Notestein, 1982: 679)—an ethnocentric and essentially imperialistic assumption. Giddens has noted the inclination among evolutionary theorists to equate the West's greater power with cultural superiority: "If the adage that might does not confer right is an old one, it is frequently forgotten by evolutionary theorists as a consequence of their very evolutionism" (1984: 242).

9. With the exception of Caldwell's insistence on the more qualitative "micro-approach" to demography (see Appendix A), the methods of world-system demography are highly technical. McNicoll (1988: 5–7) traces "the

disciplining of demography" through advances in measurement techniques such as cohort projection methods, "providing the mills for which the rapidly accumulating volume of census and registration data produced endless grist." Demeny (1988: 464) has characterized demography's research mode as "industrial," putting "a high premium on research products" that are "quantitative, standardized, replicable, and packageable for multi-country use."

10. Going so far as to characterize much of demographic research as "an oxymoron," Demeny finds in demography "strong forces that tend to relegate research to the status of an inconsequential or even counterproductive activity" (1988: 471, 467). Making a similar point, Dennis Hodgson (1988: 554) sees demographic research as "committed to a goal, not to a discipline or a method for approaching truth."

11. A smattering of critical demographic literature exists, albeit largely outside mainstream demographic debate and journals. Djurfeldt (1980) has critically analyzed India's mass vasectomy camps (see Krishnakumar 1973; Valsan 1977). Other critiques have presented family planning programs as inappropriate aspects of United States foreign policy (Demerath 1976) or as anti-Communist (Banerji 1980; Bondestam 1980) or racist (Gray 1980) or coercive and ethnocentric (Hartmann 1987; Warwick 1982).

Bibliography

Quotations from the Changing African Family–Nigeria documents, in eleven bound volumes housed at the Department of Demography, Research School of Social Sciences, Australian National University, Canberra (described by data category in Appendix A and by volume content in Appendix B), are cited in the text as follows:

CAFN1 Block Reports (see Appendix B, #1) and CAFN2 Daily Reports (Appendix B, #41) by page number (e.g., CAFN1-br: p. 12; CAFN-dr: p. 36);

CAFN2 and CAFN3 Final Notes (see Appendix B, #46, #50) and CAFN2 selected responses (Appendix B, #42) by questionnaire/respondent number (e.g., CAFN2-fn: 1238; CAFN3-fn: 0089; CAFN2-sr: 2053);

specific items from the interview schedules by question number (e.g., CAFN2-Q.45a);

all other material from the documents by the number under which it is listed in Appendix B.

Adelugba, F.A.O. 1973. "The Changing African Family Structure—An International Research Project: An Interviewer's Opinion." Final document in CAFN, vol. 1.

Ajisafe, A. K. 1924. *The Laws and Customs of the Yoruba People*. London: Routledge.

Ajuwon, Bade. 1980. "The Preservation of Yoruba Tradition through Hunters' Funeral Dirges." *Africa* 50 (1): 66–72.

Akintoye, S. A. 1971. *Revolution and Power Politics in Yorubaland, 1840–1893*. London: Longman.

Akinyele, I. B. 1946. *The Outlines of Ibadan History*. Lagos: Alebiosu Printing Press.

Amin, Samir. 1976. *Unequal Development: An Essay on the Social Formations of Peripheral Capitalism*. Sussex, Eng.: Harvester Press.

Arikpo, Okoi. 1967. *The Development of Modern Nigeria*. Baltimore, Md.: Penguin Books.

Arnold, Fred, et al. 1975. *The Value of Children: A Cross-National Study*. Vol. 1. Honolulu: East-West Center.

Asante, Molefi Kete. 1987. *The Afrocentric Idea*. Philadelphia: Temple University Press.

Ayandele, E. A. 1974. *The Educated Elite in the Nigerian Society*. Ibadan: Ibadan University Press.

Banerji, Dababar. 1980. "Political Economy of Population Control in India." Pp. 83–101 in Lars Bondestam and Staffan Bergstron, eds., *Poverty and Population Control*. London: Academic Press.

Barber, Karin. 1981. "How Man Makes God in West Africa: Yoruba Attitudes towards the Orisa." *Africa* 51 (3): 724–45.

Bascom, William. 1969 [1937]. *The Yoruba of Southwestern Nigeria*. New York: Holt, Rinehart & Winston.

Becker, Gary S. 1960. "An Economic Analysis of Fertility." Pp. 209–40 in *Demographic and Economic Change in Developed Countries*. Princeton, N.J.: Princeton University Press.

———. 1965. "A Theory of the Allocation of Time." *Economic Journal* 75 (299): 493–517.

Behar, Cem L. 1987. "Malthus and the Development of Demographic Analysis." *Population Studies* 41:269–81.

Berelson, Bernard. 1967. "The Population Council Communication Suitcase." Pp. 168–70 in Donald J. Bogue, ed., *Mass Communication and Motivation for Birth Control*. University of Chicago: Community and Family Studies Center.

Berger, Peter L., and Thomas Luckman. 1966. *The Social Construction of Reality*. New York: Doubleday.

Berrio, Diego, and Antholy A. Hudgins. 1990. "Issues in Family Planning Clinic Management in Six Latin American Countries." Paper presented to the annual meeting of the Population Association of America, Toronto.

Biobaku, S. O. 1959. "The Problem of Traditional History with Special Reference to Yoruba Traditions." *Journal of Historical Society of Nigeria* 1 (1): 26–43.

———. 1973. *Sources of Yoruba History*. Oxford: Clarendon Press.

Birdsall, Nancy. 1982. "Fertility and Development." Pp. 241–47 in John A. Ross, ed., *International Encyclopedia of Population*. New York: Free Press.

Blake, Judith. 1968. "Are Babies Consumer Durables? A Critique of Economic Theory of Reproductive Motivation." *Population Studies* 22:5–25.

Blau, Peter M. 1964. *Exchange and Power in Social Life*. New York: Wiley.

Bleek, Wolf. 1987. "Lying Informants: A Fieldwork Experience from Ghana." *Population and Development Review* 13:314–22.

Blumer, Herbert. 1969. *Symbolic Interactionism: Perspective and Method*. Englewood Cliffs, N.J.: Prentice-Hall.

Bollen, Kenneth A. 1983. "World System Position, Dependency, and Democracy: The Cross-National Evidence." *American Sociological Review* 48:468–79.

Bondestam, Lars. 1980. "The Political Ideology of Population Control." Pp. 1–38 in Lars Bondestam and Staffan Bergstrom, eds., *Poverty and Population Control*. London: Academic Press.

Bondestam, Lars, and Staffan Bergstrom, eds., 1980. *Poverty and Population Control*. London: Academic Press.

Bongaarts, John. 1978. "A Framework for Analyzing the Proximate Determinants of Fertility." *Population and Development Review* 4:105–32.

Bornschier, Volker, and Christopher Chase-Dunn. 1985. *Transnational Corporations and Underdevelopment*. New York: Praeger.

Bourdieu, Pierre. 1977. *Outline of a Theory of Practice*. Trans. Richard Nice. London: Cambridge University Press.

Bourgeois-Pichat, Jean. 1973. *Main Trends in Demography*. London: Allen & Unwin.

Brackett, James W. 1968. "The Evolution of Marxist Theories of Population: Marxism Recognizes the Population Problem." *Demography* 5:158–73.

Bradshaw, York W. 1985. "Dependent Development in Black Africa: A Cross-National Study." *American Sociological Review* 50:195–207.

———. 1988. "Reassessing Economic Dependency and Uneven Development: The Kenyan Experience." *American Sociological Review* 53:693–708.

Braithwaite, John. 1984. *Corporate Crime in the Pharmaceutical Industry*. London: Routledge & Kegan Paul.

Buchanan, K. M., and J. C. Pugh. 1955. *Land and People in Nigeria: The Human Geography of Nigeria and Its Environmental Background*. London: University of London Press.

Buell, Raymond Leslie. 1928. *The Native Problem in Africa*. New York: Macmillan.

Bulatao, Rodolfo A. 1979. *On the Nature of the Transition in the Value of Children*. Papers of the East-West Population Institute no. 60-A. Honolulu: East-West Center.

———. 1980. "The Transition in the Value of Children and the Fertility Transition." Paper presented to seminar "Determinants of Fertility Trends: Major Theories and New Directions," International Union for the Scientific Study of Population, Bad Hamburg, 14–17 April.

———. 1981. "Values and Disvalues of Children in Successive Childbearing Decisions." *Demography* 18:1–25.

Bundy, McGeorge. 1984. "The United States Government and the Population Problem Abroad." *Population and Development Review* 10:505–10.

Burns, Sir Alan. 1948 [1929]. *History of Nigeria*. London: Allen & Unwin.

———. 1957. *In Defense of Colonies*. London: Allen & Unwin.

CAFN1, CAFN2, CAFN3. See headnote.

Cain, Mead. 1982. "Perspectives on Family and Fertility in Developing Countries." *Population Studies* 36:159–75.

———. 1983. "Fertility as an Adjustment to Risk." *Population and Development Review* 9:688–702.

———. 1984. *Women's Status and Fertility in Developing Countries: Son Preference and Economic Security*. New York: Center for Policy Studies.

Caldwell, John C. 1970. "Urbanisation and Fertility Control in Tropical Africa." *African Urban Notes* 6 (1): 33–45.

———. 1973. "Family Planning in Continental Sub-Saharan Africa." Pp. 50–66 in T. E. Smith, ed., *The Politics of Family Planning in the Third World*. London: Allen & Unwin.

———. 1974. "The Study of Fertility and Fertility Change in Tropical Africa."

International Statistical Institute Occasional Papers no. 7. The Hague: World Fertility Survey.

————, ed. 1975. *Population Growth and Socioeconomic Change in West Africa.* New York: Columbia University Press.

————. 1976a. "Fertility and the Household in Nigeria." *Journal of Comparative Family Studies* 7 (2): 193–253.

————. 1976b. *The Socio-economic Explanation of High Fertility: Papers on the Yoruba Society of Nigeria.* Changing African Family Project Series, Monograph no. 1. Canberra: Australian National University Press.

————. 1976c. "Toward a Restatement of Demographic Transition Theory." *Population and Development Review* 2:321–66.

————. 1977a. "The Economic Rationality of High Fertility: An Investigation Illustrated with Nigerian Survey Data." *Population Studies* 31:5–27.

————., ed. 1977b. *The Persistence of High Fertility: Population Prospects in the Third World.* Family and Fertility Change: Changing African Family Companion Series, no. 1. Canberra: Australian National University Press.

————. 1979a. "Education as a Factor in Mortality Decline: An Examination of Nigerian Data." *Population Studies* 33:395–413.

————. 1979b. "Marriage, the Family and Fertility in Sub-Saharan Africa with Special Reference to Research Programmes in Ghana and Nigeria." Pp. 359–72 in S. A. Huzayyin and G. T. Acsadi, eds., *Family and Marriage in Some African and Asiatic Countries.* Research Monograph no. 6. Cairo: Cairo Demographic Centre.

————. 1980. "Mass Education as a Determinant of the Timing of Fertility Decline." *Population and Development Review* 6:225–55.

————. 1981a. "Fertility in Africa." Pp. 97–118 in Nick Eberstadt, ed., *Fertility Decline in the Less Developed Countries.* New York: Praeger.

————. 1981b. "The Mechanisms of Demographic Change in Historical Perspective." *Population Studies* 35:5–27.

————. 1981c. "Perspectives on Fertility and Mortality in Africa." Pp. 32–48 in United Nations Economic Commission for Africa, *Population Dynamics: Fertility and Mortality in Africa.* Addis Ababa: ECA.

————. 1982a. "The Failure of Theories of Social and Economic Change to Explain Demographic Change: Puzzles of Modernization or Westernization." *Research in Population Economics* 4:297–332.

————. 1982b. *Theory of Fertility Decline.* London: Academic Press.

————. 1988a. "The Origins and Development of Demography as a Social Science." Paper presented to seminar "Ideas of Social Science," Australian National University, Canberra, 12–13 March.

————. 1988b. "The Shadow of the Future." The 1988 Madgwick Lecture, University of New England. Department of Demography, Australian National University. Photocopy.

Caldwell, John C., and Pat Caldwell. 1976. "Demographic and Contraceptive Innovators: A Study of Transitional African Society." *Journal of Biosocial Science* 8 (4): 347–65.

———. 1977. "The Role of Marital Sexual Abstinence in Determining Fertility: A Study of the Yoruba in Nigeria." *Population Studies* 31:193–217.

———. 1978. "The Achieved Small Family: Early Fertility Transition in an African City." *Studies in Family Planinng* 9 (1): 2–18.

———. 1981a. "Cause and Sequence in the Reduction of Post-Natal Abstinence in Ibadan City, Nigeria." Pp. 181–99 in Hilary J. Page and Ron Lesthaeghe, eds., *Child-spacing in Tropical Africa: Traditions and Change*. London: Academic Press.

———. 1981b. "The Function of Child-spacing in Traditional Societies, and the Direction of Change." Pp. 73–92 in Hilary J. Page and Ron Lesthaeghe, ed., *Child-spacing in Tropical Africa: Traditions and Change*. London: Academic Press.

———. 1983. "The Demographic Evidence for the Incidence and Cause of Abnormally Low Fertility in Tropical Africa." *World Health Statistics Quarterly* 36 (1): 2–33.

———. 1985. *Cultural Forces Tending to Sustain High Fertility in Tropical Africa*. Washington, D.C.: World Bank, Population, Health, and Nutrition Department.

———. 1986. *Limiting Population Growth and the Ford Foundation Contribution*. London: Frances Pinter.

———. 1987. "The Cultural Context of High Fertility in Sub-Saharan Africa." *Population and Development Review* 13:409–37.

———. 1988a. "Is the Asian Family Planning Program Model Suited to Africa?" *Studies in Family Planning* 19 (1): 19–28.

———. 1988b. "Marital Status and Abortion in Sub-Saharan Africa." Paper presented to seminar "Nuptiality in Sub-Saharan Africa," International Union for the Scientific Study of Population, Committee on Anthropological Demography, Paris, 14–17 November.

———. 1988c. "An Overview of the Potential and Actual Contribution of the Anthropological Approach to the Understanding of Factors Affecting Demographic Variables—Fertility, Mortality, and Migration." Paper presented to the Regional African Population Conference of the International Union for the Scientific Study of Population, Dakar, Senegal, April.

Caldwell, John C., Pat Caldwell, and Bruce Caldwell. 1987. "Anthropology and Demography: The Mutual Reinforcement of Speculation and Research." *Current Anthropology* 28 (1): 25–43.

Caldwell, John C., A. G. Hill, and Valerie J. Hull, eds. 1984. *The Micro Approach in Demographic Research*. Collected Papers from an International Union for the Scientific Study of Population seminar, Australian National University. Canberra: Australian National University Department of Demography Press.

Caldwell, John C., and Adenola Igun. 1970. "The Spread of Anti-natal Knowledge and Practice in Nigeria." *Population Studies* 24:21–34.

———. 1971. "An Experiment with Census-Type Age Enumeration in Nigeria." *Population Studies* 25:287–302.

Caldwell, John C., I. O. Orubuloye, and Pat Caldwell. 1991. "The Destabilization of the Traditional Yoruba Sexual System." *Population and Development Review* 17:229–62.

Caldwell, John C., and Helen Ware. 1977. "The Evolution of Family Planning in an African City: Ibadan, Nigeria." *Population Studies* 31:487–507.

Chamberlain, Neil W. 1974. *Beyond Malthus: Population and Power*. Englewood Cliffs, N.J.: Prentice-Hall.

Chase-Dunn, Christopher. 1975. "The Effects of International Economic Dependence on Development and Inequality: A Cross-National Study." *American Sociological Review* 40:720–38.

Chirot, Daniel, and Thomas D. Hall. 1982. "World System Theory." Pp. 81–106 in Ralph Turner and James Short, eds., *Annual Review of Sociology*, vol. 8. Palo Alto: Annual Reviews.

Christian Council of Nigeria. 1965. *Family Planning in Christian Marriage*. Christian Home and Family Life Book no. 8. Ibadan: Daystar Press.

Cicourel, Aaron V. 1974. *Theory and Method in a Study of Argentine Fertility*. New York: Wiley.

Clapperton, Hugh. 1829. *Journal of a Second Expedition into the Interior of Africa*. London: John Murray.

Cleland, John. 1985. "Marital Fertility Decline in Developing Countries—Theories and the Evidence." Pp. 204–329 in John Cleland and John Hobcraft, eds., *Reproductive Change in Developing Countries*. London: Oxford University Press.

Cleland, John, and C. Wilson. 1987. "Demand Theories of the Fertility Transition: An Iconoclastic View." *Population Studies* 41:5–30.

Coale, Ansley J. 1973. "The Demographic Transition." Pp. 53–72 in *International Population Conference, Liege*, vol. 1. Liege, Belgium: International Union for the Scientific Study of Population.

Coale, Ansley J., and Edgar M. Hoover. 1958. *Population Growth and Economic Development in Low-Income Countries: A Case Study of India's Prospects*. Princeton, N.J.: Princeton University Press.

Coale, Ansley J., and T. James Trussell. 1974. "Model Fertility Schedules: Variations in the Age Structure of Child-bearing in Human Populations." *Population Index* 40 (2):185–258.

———. 1978. "Technical Note: Finding the Two Parameters That Specify a Model Schedule of Marital Fertility." *Population Index* 44 (2): 203–12.

Cogswell, Betty, and Marvin Sussman. 1979. "Family and Fertility." Pp. 180–202 in R. Burr et al., eds., *Contemporary Theories about the Family*, vol. 1: *Research Based Theory*. New York: Free Press.

Collins, Randall. 1979. *The Credential Society: An Historical Sociology of Education and Stratification*. New York: Academic Press.

Crane, Barbara B., and Jason L. Finkle. 1989. "The United States, China, and the United Nations Population Fund: Dynamics of U.S. Policymaking." *Population and Development Review* 15:23–59.

Cutright, Phillips, and Richard Adams. 1984. "Economic Dependency and Fertility in Asia and Latin America, 1960–1980." *Comparative Social Research* 7:111–32.

Cutright, Phillips, and Lowell Hargens. 1984. "The Threshold Hypothesis: Evidence from Less Developed Latin American Countries, 1950 to 1980." *Demography* 21:459–73.

Cutright, Phillips, and William R. Kelly. 1981. "The Role of Family Planning Programs in Fertility Declines in Less Developed Countries, 1958–1977." *International Family Planning Perspectives* 7:145–51.

Daly, Herman E. 1971. "A Marxian-Malthusian View of Poverty and Development." *Population Studies* 25:25–37.

Daly, Mary. 1978. *Gyn/Ecology: The Metaethics of Radical Feminism.* Boston: Beacon Press.

Davis, Kingsley, and Judith Blake. 1956. "Social Structure and Fertility: An Analytic Framework." *Economic Development and Cultural Change* 4 (3): 211–35.

Davis, Kingsley, and Wilbert E. Moore. 1945. "Some Principles of Stratification." *American Sociological Review* 10:242–49.

DeGraff, Deborah S. 1990. "Increasing Contraceptive Use in Bangladesh: The Role of Demand and Supply Factors." Paper presented to the annual meeting of the Population Association of America, Toronto.

Demeny, Paul. 1984. "A Perspective on Long-term Population Growth." *Population and Development Review* 10:103–26.

———. 1985. "Bucharest, Mexico City, and Beyond." *Population and Development Review* 11:99–106.

———. 1986. "Population and the Invisible Hand." *Demography* 23:473–88.

———. 1988. "Social Science and Population Policy." *Population and Development Review* 14:451–79.

Demerath, Nicholas J. 1976. *Birth Control and Foreign Policy: The Alternatives to Family Planning.* New York: Harper & Row.

Denzin, Normal K. 1983. "Interpretive Interactionism." Pp. 129–46 in Gareth Morgan, ed., *Beyond Method: Strategies for Social Research.* Beverly Hills, Calif.: Sage.

Djurfeldt, Goran. 1980. "Family Planning in a Tamil Village." Pp. 103–36 in Lars Bondestam and Staffan Bergstrom, eds., *Poverty and Population Control.* London: Academic Press.

Dowie, Mark. 1979. "The Corporate Crime of the Century." *Mother Jones,* November, pp. 23–49.

Dyck, Arthur J. 1982. "Ethics." Pp. 183–88 in John A. Ross, ed., *International Encyclopedia of Population.* New York: Free Press.

Eades, J. S. 1980. *The Yoruba Today.* Cambridge: Cambridge University Press.

Easterlin, Richard A. 1975. "An Economic Framework for Fertility Analysis." *Studies in Family Planning* 6 (3): 54–63.

———. 1978. "The Economics and Sociology of Fertility: A Synthesis." Pp. 57–133 in Charles Tilly, ed., *Historical Studies of Changing Fertility.* Princeton, N.J.: Princeton University Press.

Easterlin, Richard A., and Eileen M. Crimmins. 1985. *The Fertility Revolution: A Supply–Demand Analysis.* Chicago: University of Chicago Press.

Elias, T. O. 1951. *Nigerian Land Law and Custom.* London: Routledge & Kegan Paul.

Emerson, Joan P. 1970. "Behavior in Private Places: Sustaining Definitions of Reality in Gynecological Examinations." Pp. 74–97 in Hans P. Dreitzel, ed., *Recent Sociology,* vol. 2: *Patterns of Communicative Behavior.* London: Collier-Macmillan.

Evans, Peter. 1979. *Dependent Development.* Princeton, N.J.: Princeton University Press.

Fadipe, N. A. 1970 [1939]. *The Sociology of the Yoruba.* Ed. and intro. F. O. Okediji and Q. O. Okediji. Ibadan: Ibadan University Press.

Faruqee, R., and R. Gulhati. 1983. *Rapid Population Growth in Sub-Saharan Africa: Issues and Policies.* World Bank Staff Working Paper 559. Washington, D.C.: World Bank.

Fawcett, James T. 1977. "The Value and Cost of Children: Converging Theory and Research." Pp. 91–114 in Lado T. Ruzicka, ed., *The Economics and Social Supports for High Fertility.* Canberra: Australian National University and Development Studies Center.

———. 1986. "The Value and Cost of Children." Pp. 65–84 in K. Mahadevan, ed., *Fertility and Mortality: Theory, Methodology, and Empirical Issues.* Beverly Hills, Calif.: Sage.

Fawcett, James T., et al. 1974. *The Value of Children in Asia and the United States: Comparative Perspectives.* Papers of the East-West Population Institute, no. 32. Honolulu: East-West Center.

Federal Republic of Nigeria. 1985. "National Policy on Population for Development, Unity, Progress, and Self-Reliance." November. Mimeo.

Festinger, Leon. 1966 [1957]. *A Theory of Cognitive Dissonance.* Stanford, Calif.: Stanford University Press.

Finkle, Jason L., and Barbara B. Crane. 1985. "Ideology and Politics at Mexico City: The United States at the 1984 International Conference on Population." *Population and Development Review* 11:1–23.

Forbes, D. K. 1984. *The Geography of Underdevelopment.* London: Croom Helm.

Foucault, Michel. 1975. *Discipline and Punish: The Birth of the Prison.* Trans. Allen Lane. London: Penguin Books.

Frank, A. G. 1969. *Latin America: Underdevelopment or Revolution.* New York: Monthly Review Press.

———. 1979. *Mexican Agriculture, 1521–1630: Transformations of the Mode of Production.* Cambridge: Cambridge University Press.

Freedman, Ronald. 1982. "Fertility Decline: Theories." Pp. 248–66 in John A. Ross, ed., *International Encyclopedia of Population.* New York: Free Press.

———. 1986. "Theories of Fertility Decline." Pp. 30–36 in K. Mahadevan, ed., *Fertility and Mortality: Theory, Methodology, and Empirical Issues.* Beverly Hills, Calif.: Sage.

Freeman, Peter. 1977. "The Environment and Large-Scale Water Resources Projects." Report prepared for the International Institute for Environment and Development in preparation for the United Nations Water Conference, March.

Frobenius, Leo. 1913. *The Voice of Africa.* London: Cassell Press.

Fuglesang, Andreas. 1984. "The Myth of People's Ignorance." *Development Dialogue 1984* 1–2:42–62.

George, Susan. 1977. *How the Other Half Dies: The Real Reasons for World Hunger.* New York: Penguin Books.

Giddens, Anthony. 1971. *Capitalism and Modern Social Theory: An Analysis of the Writings of Marx, Durkheim, and Max Weber.* Cambridge: Cambridge University Press.

———. 1976. *New Rules of Sociological Method.* New York: Basic Books.

———. 1979. *Central Problems in Social Theory.* London: Macmillan.

———. 1984. *The Constitution of Society: Outline of the Theory of Structuration.* Berkeley: University of California Press.

———. 1987. *Social Theory and Modern Sociology.* Stanford, Calif: Stanford University Press.

Glaser, Barney G., and Anselm L. Strauss. 1967. *The Discovery of Grounded Theory: Strategies for Qualitative Research.* Chicago: Aldine.

Goffman, Erving. 1959. *The Presentation of Self in Everyday Life.* New York: Doubleday.

———. 1971. *Relations in Public: Microstudies of the Public Order.* New York: Penguin Books.

———. 1974. *Frame Analysis: An Essay on the Organization of Experience.* New York: Harper & Row.

Goliber, Thomas J. 1989. "Africa's Expanding Population: Old Problems, New Policies." *Population Bulletin* 44 (3).

Gordon, Linda. 1976. *Woman's Body, Woman's Right.* New York: Grossman.

Gray, Madi. 1980. "U.S. Population Policies, Development, and the Rural Poor in Africa." *Journal of Modern African Studies* 20 (1): 45–67.

Grebnik, E. 1989. "Demography, Democracy, and Demonology." *Population and Development Review* 15:1–22.

Greenhalgh, Susan. 1990. "Toward a Political Economy of Fertility: Anthropological Contributions." Population Council Working Paper no. 12.

Gutkind, Peter C. W., and Immanuel Wallerstein, eds. 1976. *The Political Economy of Contemporary Africa.* Beverly Hills, Calif.: Sage.

Hair, Paul. 1982. "Children in Society: 1850–1980." Pp. 34–61 in Theodore Barker and Michael Drake, eds., *Population and Society in Britain, 1850–1980.* New York: New York University Press.

Handwerker, W. Penn. 1986. *Culture and Reproduction: An Anthropological Critique of Demographic Transition Theory.* Boulder, Colo.: Westview Press.

Hartmann, Betsy. 1987. *Reproductive Rights and Wrongs: The Global Politics of Population Control and Contraceptive Choice.* New York: Harper & Row.

Hawthorn, Geoffrey. 1970. *The Sociology of Fertility.* London: Collier-Macmillan.

Hermalin, Albert I. 1986. "Some Observations on the Regulation of Fertility." Pp. 55–64 in K. Mahadevan, ed., *Fertility and Mortality: Theory, Methodology, and Empirical Issues.* Beverly Hills, Calif.: Sage.

Hodgson, Dennis. 1983. "Demography as Social Science and Policy Science." *Population and Development Review* 9:1–34.

————. 1988. "Orthodoxy and Revisionism in American Demography." *Population and Development Review* 14:541–69.

Hoffman, Lois Wladis, and Martin L. Hoffman. 1973. "The Value of Children to Parents." Pp. 19–76 in James T. Fawcett, ed., *Psychological Perspectives on Population.* New York: Basic Books.

Hofsten, Erland. 1980. "Bucharest and After." Pp. 213–21 in Lars Bondestam and Staffan Bergstrom, eds., *Poverty and Population Control.* London: Academic Press.

Homans, George C. 1961. *Social Behavior: Its Elementary Forms.* New York: Harcourt, Brace & World.

Hout, Michael. 1980. "Trade Dependence and Fertility in Hispanic America: 1900–1975." Chap. 8 in A. Bergesen, ed., *Studies of the Modern World System.* New York: Academic Press.

Ifemesia, C. C. 1978. *Southeastern Nigeria in the Nineteenth Century: An Introductory Analysis.* New York: NOK Publishers.

Inkeles, Alex, and David H. Smith. 1974. *Becoming Modern: Individual Change in Six Developing Countries.* London: Heinemann Educational Books.

Isichei, Elizabeth. 1983. *A History of Nigeria.* London: Longman.

Isiugo-Abanihe, Uche C. 1985. "Child Fosterage in West Africa." *Population and Development Review* 11:53–73.

Jaffee, David. 1985. "Export Dependence and Economic Growth: A Reformulation and Respecification." *Social Forces* 64:102–17.

Jamal, Amir H. 1984. "The Cultural Dimensions of Development: National Cultural Values versus Transnational Cultural Domination." *Development Dialogue 1984* 1–2:76–82.

Johansson, S. Ryan. 1991. " 'Implicit' Policy and Fertility during Development." *Population and Development Review* 17:377–414.

Johnson, Samuel. 1966 [1921]. *The History of the Yorubas: From the Earliest Times to the Beginning of the Protectorate.* London: Routledge & Kegan Paul.

Kabwegyere, T., and J. Mbula. 1979. *A Case of the Akamba of Eastern Kenya.* Canberra: Australian National University Press.

Kantner, John F. 1982. "Population, Policy, and Political Atavism." *Demography* 19:429–38.

Kasarda, John D., John O. G. Billy, and Kirsten West. 1986. *Status Enhancement and Fertility: Reproductive Responses to Social Mobility and Educational Opportunity.* New York: Academic Press.

Keyfitz, Nathan. 1985. *Applied Mathematical Demography.* 2d ed. New York: Springer-Verlag.

Kiernan, V. G. 1969. *The Lords of Human Kind: European Attitudes toward the Outside World in the Imperial Age.* London: Weidenfeld & Nicolson.

Kilbride, Philip Leroy, and Janet Capriotti Kilbride. 1990. *Changing Family Life in East Africa: Women and Children at Risk.* University Park: Pennsylvania State University Press.

Knodel, John. 1974. *The Decline of Fertility in Germany, 1871–1939.* Princeton, N.J.: Princeton University Press.

———. 1977. "Family Limitation and the Fertility Transition: Evidence from the Age Patterns of Fertility in Europe and Asia." *Population Studies* 31:219–49.

———. 1983. "Natural Fertility: Age Patterns, Levels, and Trends." Pp. 61–102 in Rodolfo A. Bulatao and Ronald D. Lee, eds., *Determinants of Fertility in Developing Countries.* New York: Academic Press.

Knodel, John, and Etienne van de Walle. 1979. "Lessons from the Past: Policy Implications of Historical Fertility Studies." *Population and Development Review* 5:217–45.

Krishnakumar, S. 1973. "Kerala's Pioneering Experiment in Massive Vasectomy Camps." *Studies in Family Planning* 3 (8): 177–85.

Kuhn, Thomas S. 1970. *The Structure of Scientific Revolutions.* 2d ed. Chicago: University of Chicago Press.

Lee, J. M. 1967. *Colonial Development and Good Government.* Oxford: Clarendon Press.

Lee, Ronald D., and Rodolfo A. Bulatao. 1983. "The Demand for Children: A Critical Essay." Pp. 233–87 in Rodolfo A. Bulatao and Ronald D. Lee, eds., *Determinants of Fertility in Developing Countries.* New York: Academic Press.

Leibenstein, Harvey. 1974. "An Interpretation of the Economic Theory of Fertility: Promising Path or Blind Alley?" *Journal of Economic Literature* 12 (2): 457–79.

———. 1975. "The Economic Theory of Fertility Decline." *Quarterly Journal of Economics* 89 (1): 1–31.

Lesthaeghe, Ron. 1983. "A Century of Demographic and Cultural Change in Western Europe: An Exploration of Underlying Dimensions." *Population and Development Review* 9:411–35.

Levine, David. 1977. *Family Fertility in an Age of Nascent Capitalism.* London: Academic Press.

———. 1986. "The Decline of Fertility in Europe: Review Symposium." *Population and Development Review* 12:335–40.

Lewis, Gary, S. Matlomelo, T. Maliehe, and M. Sakoane. 1990. "A Focus Group Study of Contraceptive Dropouts in Lesotho." Paper presented to the annual meeting of the Population Association of America, Toronto.

Lloyd, P. C. 1962. *Yoruba Land Law.* Ibadan: Nigerian Institute of Social and Economic Research, Oxford University Press.

London, Bruce. 1988. "Dependence, Distorted Development, and Fertility Trends in Noncore Nations: A Structural Analysis of Cross-National Data." *American Sociological Review* 53:606–18.

McIntyre, W. David. 1967. *The Imperial Frontier in the Tropics, 1865–75.* London: Macmillan.

McNamara, Regina. 1982. "Demographic Transition Theory." Pp. 146–47 in John A. Ross, ed., *International Encyclopedia of Population.* New York: Free Press.

McNamara, Regina, T. McGinn, M. Wawer, and D. Lauro. 1990. "Program Evaluation in Sub-Saharan Africa: What Works and What Doesn't." Paper presented to the annual meeting of the Population Association of America, Toronto.

McNicoll, Geoffrey. 1975. "Community-level Population Policy: An Exploration." *Population and Development Review* 1:1–21.

——. 1980. "Institutional Determinants of Fertility Change." *Population and Development Review* 6:441–62.

——. 1988. "The International Union for the Scientific Study of Population and Population Policy Research." Paper presented to the Expert Group Meeting on the International Transmission of Population Policy Experience, International Union for the Scientific Study of Population, New York, 27–30 June.

Mamdani, Mahmood. 1972. *The Myth of Population Control: Family, Caste, and Class in an Indian Village.* New York: Monthly Review Press.

Marx, Karl. 1912. *Capital: A Critical Analysis of Capitalist Production.* Trans. from 3d German ed., Samuel Moore and Edward Aveling; ed. Frederick Engels. London: William Glaisher.

Mason, Karen Oppenheim. 1992. "Culture and the Fertility Transition." Paper presented at the Population Association of America Annual Meeting, April 30–May 2, Denver.

Mauldin, W. Parker, and Bernard Berelson. 1978. "Conditions of Fertility Decline in Developing Countries, 1965–75." *Studies in Family Planning* 9 (5): 89–147.

Maunier, René. 1949. *The Sociology of Colonies: An Introduction to the Study of Race Contact.* London: Routledge & Kegan Paul.

Meeker, B. F. 1981. "Fertility Decision-making Theories in Interpersonal Behaviour." Pp. 23–42 in T. K. Burch, ed., *Demographic Behaviour: Interdisciplinary Perspectives on Decision Making.* AAAS Selected Symposium 45. Boulder, Colo: Westview Press.

Mills, C. Wright. 1959. *The Sociological Imagination.* New York: Oxford University Press.

Moen, Elizabeth. 1987. "What Does 'Control over Our Bodies' Really Mean?" Pp. 277–87 in Scott W. Menard and Elizabeth W. Moen, eds., *Perspectives on Population: An Introduction to Concepts and Issues.* New York: Oxford University Press.

Mott, Frank, and Susan Mott. 1980. "Kenya's Record Population Growth: A Dilemma of Development." *Population Bulletin* 35:3–42.

Mullins, Nicholas C. 1973. *Theories and Theory Groups in Contemporary American Sociology.* New York: Harper & Row.

Nachman, Steven R. 1984. "Lies My Informants Told Me." *Journal of Anthropological Research* 40 (3): 536–55.

Namboodiri, N. Krishnan. 1986. "Societal Development and Population Change: A Reappraisal of Selected Theories." Pp. 37–54 in K. Mahadevan, ed., *Fertility and Mortality: Theory, Methodology, and Empirical Issues.* Beverly Hills, Calif.: Sage.

Nelson, Richard R. 1956. "A Theory of the Low-level Equlibrium Trap in Underdeveloped Economies." *American Economic Review* 46 (5): 894–908.

Newell, Colin. 1988. *Methods and Models in Demography.* New York: Guilford Press.

"Nigeria." 1991. Pp. 2004–25 in *The Europa World Year Book.* Vol. 2. London: Europa Publications.

"Nigeria DHS Survey Provides Much-Needed National/Regional Data." 1992. *Demographic and Health Surveys Newsletter* 5 (1): 3.

Nolan, Patrick D. 1983. "Status in the World System, Income Inequality, and Economic Growth." *American Journal of Sociology* 89:410–19.

———. 1984. "Structural Explanations of Fertility Change: The Demographic Transition, Economic Status of Women, and the World System." *Comparative Social Research* 8:81–109.

———. 1988. "World System Status, Techno-Economic Heritage, and Fertility." *Sociological Focus* 21 (1): 9–33.

Nolan, Patrick D., and Gerhard Lenski. 1985. "Techno-economic Heritage, Patterns of Development, and the Advantage of Backwardness." *Social Forces* 64:341–58.

Nolan, Patrick D., and Ralph B. White. 1983. "Demographic Differentials in the World System: A Research Note." *Social Forces* 62:1–8.

Notestein, Frank W. 1982. "Demography in the United States: A Partial Account of the Development of the Field." *Population and Development Review* 8:651–87.

O'Hear, Ann. 1986. "Pottery Making in Ilorin: A Study of the Decorated Water Cooler." *Africa* 56 (2): 175–92.

Ojo, G.J.A. 1966. *Yoruba Culture*. London: University of London Press.

Okediji, Francis Olu, John Caldwell, Pat Caldwell, and Helen Ware. 1976. "The Changing African Family Project: A Report with Special Reference to the Nigerian Segment." *Studies in Family Planning* 7 (5): 126–36.

Omran, Abdel. 1977. "Epidemiologic Transition in the U.S." *Population Bulletin* 32:1–45.

Oppong, Christine, and Wolf Bleek. 1982. "Economic Models and Having Children: Some Evidence from Kwahu, Ghana." *Africa* 52 (4): 15–33.

Orubuloye, I. O. 1977. "Fertility, Sexual Abstinence, and Contraception among the Yoruba of Western Nigeria." Diss., Department of Demography, Australian National University, Canberra.

———. 1981. "Education and Socio-Demographic Change in Nigeria: The Western Nigerian Experience." Pp. 22–41 in Helen Ware, ed., *Women, Education, and Modernization of the Family in West Africa*. Changing African Family Project Series Monograph no. 7. Canberra: Australian National University Department of Demography Press.

Overbeek, Johannes. 1974. *History of Population Theories*. Rotterdam: Rotterdam University Press.

Page, Hilary J., and Ron Lesthaeghe, eds. 1981. *Child-spacing in Tropical Africa: Traditions and Change*. New York: Academic Press.

Pariani, Siti, D. M. Heer, and M. Van Arsdol. 1990. "Contraceptive Discontinuation in East Java, Indonesia." Paper presented to the annual meeting of the Population Association of America, Toronto.

Parsons, Talcott. 1951. *The Social System*. New York: Free Press.

———. 1966. *Societies: Evolutionary and Comparative Perspectives*. New York: Prentice-Hall.

————. 1977. *The Evolution of Societies.* Ed. and intro. Jackson Toby. Englewood Cliffs, N.J.: Prentice-Hall.

Patterson, John G., and Nanda R. Shrestha. 1988. "Population Growth and Development in the Third World: The Neocolonial Context." *Studies in Comparative International Development* 23:3–32.

Redner, Harry. 1987. *The Ends of Science.* Boulder, Colo.: Westview Press.

Riesman, Paul. 1986. "The Person and the Life Cycle in African Social Life and Thought." *African Studies Review* 29 (2): 71–138.

Ritzer, George. 1980. *Sociology: A Multiparadigm Science.* Boston: Allyn & Bacon.

Russell, Bertrand. 1985 [1929]. *Marriage and Morals.* London: Unwin Paperbacks.

Ryder, Norman B. 1983. "Fertility and Family Structure." *Population Bulletin of the United Nations* 15:15–34.

Safilios-Rothschild, Constantina. 1982. "Female Power, Autonomy, and Demographic Change in the Third World." Pp. 117–32 in Richard Anker, Mayra Buvinic, and Nadia H. Youssef, eds., *Women's Roles and Population Trends in the Third World.* London: Croom Helm.

————. 1985a. *Socioeconomic Development and the Status of Women in the Third World.* New York: Center for Policy Studies.

————. 1985b. *The Status of Women and Fertility in the Third World in the 1970–80 Decade.* New York: Center for Policy Studies.

Salamone, Frank A. 1977. "The Methodological Significance of the Lying Informant." *Anthropological Quarterly* 50 (3): 117–24.

Saunders, John. 1988. *Basic Demographic Measures.* New York: University Press of America.

Schoen, Robert. 1988. *Modeling Multigroup Populations.* New York: Plenum.

Schultz, T. Paul. 1983. Review of *Theory of Fertility Decline* by John C. Caldwell. *Population and Development Review* 9:161–68.

Schultz, Theodore W. 1971. *Investment in Human Capital: The Role of Education and of Research.* New York: Free Press.

————., ed. 1974. *Economics of the Family: Marriage, Children, and Human Capital.* Chicago: University of Chicago Press.

Schutz, Alfred. 1970. *On Phenomenology and Social Relations: Selected Writings.* Ed. and intro. Helmut R. Wagner. Chicago: University of Chicago Press.

Seccombe, Wally. 1983. "Marxism and Demography." *New Left Review* 137:22–47.

Shapiro, Thomas M. 1985. *Population Control Politics: Women, Sterilization, and Reproductive Choice.* Philadelphia: Temple University Press.

Shorter, Edward. 1976. *The Making of the Modern Family.* New York: Basic Books.

Shroyer, Trent. 1970. "Toward a Critical Theory for Advanced Industrial Society." Pp. 210–34 in Hans P. Dreitzel, ed., *Recent Sociology,* vol. 2: *Patterns of Communicative Behavior.* London: Collier Macmillan.

Simmons, Ruth, Gayl D. Ness, and George B. Simmons. 1983. "On the Institutional Analysis of Population Programs." *Population and Development Review* 9:457–75.

Simons, John. 1986. "Moral Dimensions of Fertility Variation." Paper presented to the Eleventh World Congress of Sociology, New Delhi, India, August.

Sjoberg, Gideon, ed. 1967. *Ethics, Politics, and Social Research.* Cambridge, Mass.: Schenkman.

Sjoberg, Gideon, and Roger Nett. 1968. *A Methodology for Social Research.* New York: Harper & Row.

Smith, Herbert L. 1989. "Integrating Theory and Research on the Institutional Determinants of Fertility." *Demography* 26:171–84.

Smith, Robert S. 1969. *Kingdoms of the Yoruba.* New York: Harper & Row.

Smythe, Hugh H., and Mabel M. Smythe. 1960. *The New Nigerian Elite.* Stanford, Calif.: Stanford University Press.

Snyder, David, and Edward Kick. 1979. "Structural Position in the World System and Economic Growth, 1955–1970: A Multiple Network Analysis of Transnational Interaction." *American Journal of Sociology* 84:1097–1126.

Srikantan, K. S. 1977. *The Family Planning Program in the Socioeconomic Context.* New York: Population Council.

Stephens, Richard W. 1959. *Population Pressures in Africa South of the Sahara.* Washington, D.C.: George Washington University Press.

Stolnitz, George J. 1983. "Three to Five Main Challenges to Demographic Research." *Demography* 20:415–32.

Stone, Lawrence. 1977. *The Family, Sex, and Marriage in England, 1500–1800.* New York: Academic Press.

Stonich, Susan S. 1989. "The Dynamics of Social Processes and Environmental Destruction: A Central American Case Study." *Population and Development Review* 15:269–96.

Strauss, Anselm L. 1987. *Qualitative Analysis for Social Scientists.* New York: Cambridge University Press.

Talbot, P. A. 1926. *The Peoples of Southern Nigeria: Ethnology.* London: Oxford University Press.

———. 1927. *Some Nigerian Fertility Cults.* London: Oxford University Press.

Teitelbaum, Michael S. 1975. "Relevance of Demographic Transition Theory for Developing Countries." *Science* 188:420–25.

Temple, C. L. 1918. *Native Races and Their Rulers: Sketches and Studies of Official Life and Administrative Problems in Nigeria.* Cape Town: Argus.

Thibaut, John W., and Harold H. Kelley. 1959. *The Social Psychology of Groups.* New York: Wiley.

Thompson, Warren S. 1929. "Population." *American Journal of Sociology* 34:959–75.

Townes, Brenda D., et al. 1977. "Birth Planning Values and Decisions: The Prediction of Fertility." *Journal of Applied Social Psychology* 7 (1): 73–88.

Trenchard, Esther. 1987. "Rural Women's Work in Sub-Saharan Africa and the Implications for Nutrition." Pp. 153–72 in Janet H. Momsen and Janet Townsend, eds., *Geography of Gender in the Third World.* Hutchinson: State University of New York Press.

Turchi, Boone. 1975. "Microeconomic Theories of Fertility: A Critique." *Social Forces* 54:107–25.

Uhlenberg, Peter. 1980. "Death and the Family." *Journal of Family History*, Fall, pp. 313–20.

Valsan, E. H. 1977. "Successes and Problems in Family Planning Administration: Experiences in Two Districts of Kerala, India." *Studies in Family Planning* 8 (6): 148–56.

Van de Walle, Etienne, and John Knodel. 1980. "Europe's Fertility Transition: New Evidence and Lessons for Today's Developing World." *Population Bulletin* 34 (6).

Waddell, David A. G. 1960. "Queen Anne's Government and the Slave Trade." *Caribbean Quarterly* 6 (1): 7–10.

Wallerstein, Immanuel. 1964. *The Road to Independence: Ghana and the Ivory Coast.* Paris: Mouton.

———. 1966. *Social Change: The Colonial Situation.* New York: Wiley.

———. 1974. *The Modern World-System: Capitalist Agriculture and the Origins of the European World-Economy in the Sixteenth Century.* New York: Academic Press.

———. 1979. *The Capitalist World Economy.* Cambridge: Cambridge University Press.

———. 1980. *The Modern World-System,* vol. 2: *Mercantilism and the Consolidation of the European World-Economy, 1600–1750.* New York: Academic Press.

Ward, Kathryn B. 1984. *Women in the World-System: Its Impact on Status and Fertility.* New York: Praeger.

Ware, Helen. 1975. "The Limits of Acceptable Family Size in Western Nigeria." *Journal of Biosocial Science* 7:273–96.

———. 1978. *The Economic Value of Children in Asia and Africa: Comparative Perspectives.* Papers of the East-West Population Institute, no. 50. Honolulu: East-West Center.

Warwick, Donald P. 1982. *Bitter Pills.* Cambridge: Cambridge University Press.

Weber, Max. 1958. "Science as a Vocation." Pp. 129–56 in H. H. Gerth and C. Wright Mills, eds., *From Max Weber: Essays in Sociology.* New York: Oxford University Press.

———. 1968. *Economy and Society: An Outline of Interpretive Sociology.* Trans. Ephraim Fischoff et al.; ed. Guenther Roth and Claus Wittich. New York: Bedminster Press.

Webster, J. B. 1964. *The African Churches among the Yoruba, 1888–1922.* Oxford: Clarendon Press.

Wilson, H. T. 1983. "Anti-Method as a Counterstructure in Social Research Practice." Pp. 247–59 in Gareth Morgan, ed., *Beyond Method: Strategies for Social Research.* Beverly Hills, Calif.: Sage.

Wimberly, Dale W. 1990. "Investment Dependence and Alternative Explanations of Third World Mortality: A Cross-National Study." *American Sociological Review* 55:75–91.

Woods, R. I. 1987. "Approaches to the Fertility Transition in Victorian England." *Population Studies* 41:283–311.

World Fertility Survey. 1984. *The Nigerian Fertility Survey, 1981–82*, vol. 2: *Methodology and Findings*. Voorburg, Neth.: International Statistical Institute; London: World Fertility Survey.

Zerubavel, Eviatar. 1982. "The Standardization of Time: A Sociohistorical Perspective." *American Journal of Sociology* 88:1–23.

Index

Abeokuta, 15, 27
Abiku, 87
Accra Conference, 28
Aiyetoro, 16
Akungba, 54
Aramoko-Ekiti, 42, 53
Australian National University, xiii, 4, 123

Back region, 63, 64
Bias of categorization, 77
British colonial government, 19, 20, 24; and bureaucratic surveillance, 23–26
British merchants, 21, 24
Bureaucratic surveillance, 46, 65; advancing, 23–26; compliance in, 3, 47–48, 53–54, 65, 96; and deconstruction of indigenous political economy, 25–26; defined, 2; and disciplinary power, 66–67, 96; as a historical theme in Yorubaland, 31; as integral to potential birth control enforcement, 3–4; and modernization, 3; as one CAFN lesson, 68, 76–77; as opposed to family authority, 96; and secondary-role behavior, 76–77; and social control, 96; and Yoruba respondents, 48–49, 57–58

Caldwell, Professor John C.: as director of Changing African Family–Nigeria projects, 4; and family

nucleation, 100–101, 150n2; and high fertility as reasonable, 151n7; and "micro-approach," 114, 151–52n9; and upward wealth flow, 100
Caldwell, Pat, xiii, 41, 44, 120, 127
Changing African Family–Nigeria projects (CAFN), xiii, 4–7, 17, 18, 19, 113, 117–22, 123–42, 143n4, 146nn1, 2, 3 (top); bureaucracy of, 33–46, 47; as bureaucratic surveillance, 32, 76–77; and CAFN1, 4, 5, 48, 114, 116, 117, 119, 120–21, 123–25, 126–27, 128, 131, 146n1 (top), 147n5 (top); and CAFN2, 4, 7, 14, 48, 116, 118, 119, 120, 126, 128, 129, 132–36, 146n3 (top), 147nn1– 3, 149n14; and CAFN3, 5, 7, 44, 116, 120, 121, 125, 129, 130, 131, 136–42, 146n1 (top); as cultural imposition, 97, 109; as exploitative of Yorubas, 98–99; and funding agencies, 97, 102–6; and gaining entrance, 47–65; and geographic surveillance, 47–49; as hierarchically organized, 33–34; as invading of subjects' territorial selves, 61–64; lessons inherent in, 66–78, 147– 49nn1–14; principal researchers in, 4, 40, 41–42; and question sensitivity, 60–61; and questionnaires, 50, 55, 113, 117–19, 133–35, 138– 42, 146n3 (bottom); as reactive, 98–99, 101–2; and sampling, 48; as social products, 7–8; supervisory